S0-AVT-244

ACKNOWLEDGMENTS

Dineen Miller, my sister in Christ and best designer in the world, thank you for how you pour out your talents for the Kingdom of God. Our Kingdom Conversations over the years are priceless!

Martha Bush, your love and support have held me up and walked me through many manuscripts. I love you.

Denise Harmer, editor. THANK YOU.

Adrianna Cast, thank you for your continued support of the ministry and how you love God and others well. Thank you, Lu MacDonald and Ahnee Broman, you are Kingdom Warriors!

Thank you to my loyal readers and friends who have traveled along life's journey with me. What a ride!

ENDORSEMENTS

"Lynn Donovan is a beloved daughter, fierce warrior, champion of people, encourager, intercessor, and cherished friend. She is one who steps into the battle unafraid, as she knows who she is and to whom she belongs. Lynn also carries a powerful prophetic voice. In ministry I've witnessed many times how the Lord shares his heart of love for an individual through her. Lynn has cultivated and pursues an intimate relationship with our heavenly Dad. Through her book, *Kingdom Conversations*, she allows us into her intimate conversations with God the Father, Jesus Christ, and the Holy Spirit. This is a book you will experience. You will encounter the very heart of the Father. His voice will stir your soul and spirit and as you speak the declarations your heart will arise, and you will step into greater mandates and realms of authority. There is so much more, and we have been invited in! Thank you, Lynn, for your relentless pursuit of the Holy Trinity and sharing his love with his children."

—**Lu MacDonald**, *Prophetic Art Ministries Director*

"Lynn Donovan is truly a woman after God's heart. *Kingdom Conversations* offers biblical truths and heartwarming inspiration for all seasons. You can hear the Father's love speaking through Lynn. She is a personal friend and I've never met anybody as passionate about God. This book speaks spirit to spirit."

—**Charlene Fransz**, *Freedom Prayer Ministries*

"Lynn lives out of the intimacy with her Father in heaven. Her words are poised with such delicacy, out of an overflow of the Father's Love. They cut right to the core of my being speaking his truth to my very soul. Lynn thank you for living out of the Father's heart. My spirit is encouraged and uplifted within me, made ready to mount up with wings like eagles, to run and not grow weary to walk and not grow faint!"

—Natalie Mimless

"Can you imagine having an intimate conversation with God? Lynn Donovan did on the pages of this devotional book. Instead of a conversation, you might say this book is a monologue with God being the only one talking. As God spoke, Lynn listened, and wrote down what he was saying to her in her personal journal. As I read, I could hear God speaking to me, too, about my dreams, hurts, plans for my life, encouragement, and all that I have need of. At the end of each devotion, Lynn's gifted penmanship clearly shines through with prayers straight from her heart. This 90-day devotion will leave you wanting another devotional book by Lynn."

—Martha Bush, Author of *Helping Hurting Children: A Journey of Healing,* Contributor: *Winning Them With Prayer, SpirituallyUnequalMarriage.com, and Lynndonovan.com*

"This book made me smile from ear to ear. It is a precious thing to be a friend of God and to hear his heart. As a ministry partner with Lynn, I know the degree to which she has pressed on to know Jesus, Holy Spirit, and the Father, and this book is fruit of that. Having read these devotions, I believe any reader who marinates in these words day-by-day will be changed. The heart of the Father blows from its pages giving us love notes to be received. Read, and be greatly encouraged and strengthened!"

—Ann Hutchison, *Director*, Spirituallyunequalmarriage.com

To every child of God who hungers and thirsts for more.
You shall be satisfied! Blessed are those who hunger and
thirst for righteousness, for they will be filled.

— MATTHEW 5:6

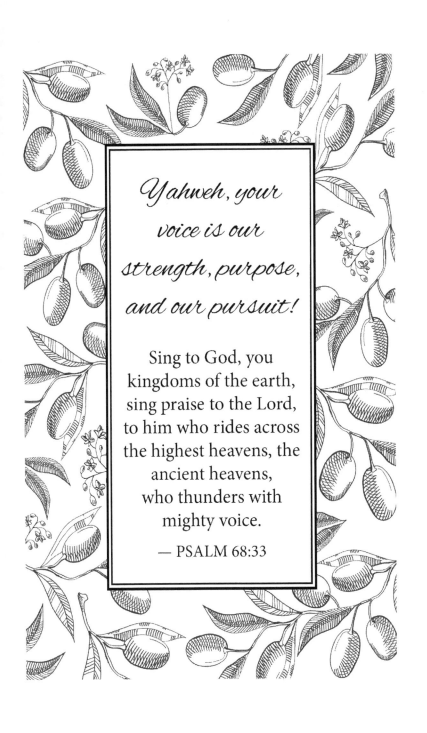

Yahweh, your voice is our strength, purpose, and our pursuit!

Sing to God, you kingdoms of the earth, sing praise to the Lord, to him who rides across the highest heavens, the ancient heavens, who thunders with mighty voice.

— PSALM 68:33

MEET LYNN

*Take delight in the Lord, and he will give
you the desires of your heart.*
PSALM 37:4

My friend, I'm a sold-out, on fire, Jesus follower. It's my daily purpose to pursue God, the Father, Jesus Christ, and live in cooperation with the Holy Spirit. I'm also a wife, a mom, a pastor, and a woman of prayer. I grew up in church. However, as a young adult in my twenties, I ran away from my childhood faith and found myself living a messed-up, fast-paced, and ugly lifestyle. My years in the Prodigal Badlands introduced me to my husband, who didn't know God. We quickly married and started a family. It was in the third year of our marriage that I realized that I missed the Lord. He beckoned me to return to my childhood faith. That was when this prodigal daughter ran home into the open arms of my heavenly Father.

Fast forward to the writing of this book, my husband and I have been married for nearly three decades. And by the grace of God, my husband stepped into the Kingdom on March 14, 2019. He was baptized on our 27th wedding anniversary, a sweet gift from my Father in Heaven. However, for an exceptionally long time, I lived out my faith within a spiritually mismatched home.

In 2006 I began an online ministry to serve others who are also married to unbelievers. Through the website spirituallyunequalmarriage.com, I've been writing to encourage believers who desire to honor God, their spouse, and marriage covenant. This ministry remains near and dear to my heart. I'm thankful for all who join me online as well as the many who find encouragement reading my books, that are specific to spiritually mismatched marriages and parenting. You can find information about this ministry at the end of the book.

My marriage was the cradle that birthed my authentic faith and led me into a consuming and intimate love relationship with the Trinity. The love of God and the church is at the heart of all my ministry.

My faith life has matured over the years, and today I choose to live every day in the playground of the Holy Spirit. I also study with expectancy in the classroom of Wisdom and Revelation where Jesus instructs and the Holy Spirit leads. You might find me any day of the week somewhere riding upon the Kingdom teeter-totter bouncing between wonderment and the holy, to the silly and outlandish. And I'm always sheltered under the steady hand of our good Father, the Creator of life.

Living in his Presence and listening to his voice has become my daily pursuit. And from the depths of my heart, I yearn for every child of God to encounter and experience the mysteries, the marvels, and the miraculous that is his voice.

I bless you as you linger in the words of each devotion. I pray that you will hear the voice of our Lord. I pray your heart is moved by his love and that you step deeply into intimacy with the Trinity. I bless you to view yourself through the lens of the

Father's love as the devotions speak to your heart and develop your faith and character.

Thank you for allowing me to spend time with you. I'm deeply humbled and grateful.

May your heart, hopes, dreams, and faith-life become a playground for the Holy Spirit. And may you walk in bold and remarkable faith, in the powerful name of Jesus Christ. AMEN

He rewards those who earnestly seek him. —Hebrews 11:6b

INTRODUCTION

Over a three-year period, during my morning prayer time I would sit quietly and listen as the Lord spoke to me. His voice wasn't loud or booming, nor a burning bush, but a whisper of familiarity and love that I've learned to tune in and perceive. I would read the Word, pause, then focus on his whispers of love, affirmation, and instruction that he spoke to my heart. His voice offered direction and confirmation; my soul became filled with truth and encouragement.

Each morning I sat readied with my pen poised and I captured his voice and wrote down his whispers. I began sharing what he was speaking to me through social media. Thousands would read the devotions. They would post comments and email me that they experienced healing and Godly direction for their current circumstances. The readers found new hope and still others shared that they were motivated and encouraged in their faith. They felt loved and seen by God.

Inspired by his messages, one summer morning while standing in my garage, sensing the Holy Spirit's urging, I telephoned our local newspaper, *The Valley News*. I queried the editor about sharing what the Lord was imparting to me as a faith devotion with the readership of the newspaper. Surprisingly and with great enthusiasm, the editor agreed.

I began submitting the devotions for publication. For nearly two years the newspaper published the words of the Lord. Believers and unbelievers read them every two weeks.

I received many notes and emails thanking me for sharing the words of the Lord. I remember attending a neighborhood get-together and a friend mentioned that she read each one and they spoke to her heart. She relayed a story of how she took some homemade soup to a friend who was ill and enclosed a devotion clipped from the newspaper.

The devotions became a strength to many.

The majority of the devotions are a collection of writings that reflect the direct voice of the Father. Some are also a creation of my prayers and petitions to God. Others are personal reflections upon scripture and events in the lives of believers. Allow the Holy Spirit to lead you to discern the voice that speaks and then join your heart to the message.

The devotions reflect a scripture verse or passage as well as a prayer to pray aloud in response.

Read the devotions and sit with your pen poised over paper. Start your own Kingdom Conversations journal. Ask the Lord to speak to you. Then ask him questions. The Lord desires communication. Asking questions of God is a pathway into greater intimacy.

It's my prayer that as you read the devotions, your spiritual ears will also discern the voice of our good Father. He is kind and full of mercy and unending grace toward his children. He desires to prosper us and for us to know him intimately and to hear him speak.

I bless you to be filled with fresh revelation of his unending love and to have an experiential encounter with his presence, for that is his desire. In Jesus' name.

Walk with the Keys to the Kingdom!

DEVOTIONS FOR THE HUNGRY IN CHRIST

1

THE POWER OF WORDS

 In the beginning was the Word, and the Word was with God, and the Word was God.

JOHN 1:1

Nothing exists outside of my WORD. My voice is power. My voice is truth. My voice releases recompense, victory, and unending grace... My voice is life and love.

My people are destroyed for lack of knowledge (Hosea 4:6).

My children have a voice. Their words wield great power as my holy Scriptures declare: *Death and life are in the power of the tongue* (Proverbs 18:21). Yet, my children are unaware they have traded their voice for a facade of security and small living. The enemy has stolen their voice and corrupted their ability to change their circumstances.

It is time for the Acts 2 church to arise. I have decreed restoration of the voice of my people in this season.

Young, old, sons, daughters, mothers and fathers, widows and families, all peoples from every nation. Now is the time to regain the anointed Words and speak out, shout out, my purposes into lives and hearts of the people on earth. The time is NOW. Watch and behold, I establish restoration, breakthrough, peace, and abundance upon my people. As you pray, speak words of life and love upon yourself, your family, and others. Bless the many, and do not curse.

Praise, affirm, and lift up your efforts, your intentions before me. Create with your words a perpetual spring of Living Water flowing into the works of your hands and into the lives of those around you. Retrain your brain! Capture thoughts of doom, regret, shame, fear, lust, and all bitter lies of my enemy. Take them captive to my Son, Christ Jesus, who is purposed to destroy them. Say aloud: *I take this thought captive to Christ*. Persistence in the practice will result in a continual triumph over thoughts birthed of the enemy. Arise with words of love, praise, goodness, and words inspired by my Holy Spirit.

Today, I restore your voice unto you.

Receive this truth and walk in it.

Today, I bestow unto you the keys of the Kingdom. The keys grant access to open the treasuries of heaven through your words. Speak up. Speak out. You are children of the Most High God.

*Father, thank you for your truth. Thank you for the Word. I take back my voice and I will use it to bring hope and love to those who I encounter in my day. I reject the voice of trouble, fear, insecurity, and darkness. I choose to speak words of life. Speak through me, Father, in this season of **The Bride** to bring love, hope, and peace into the world. AMEN*

THE BLESSINGS OF SMALL BEGINNINGS

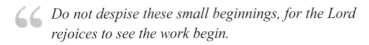

> *Do not despise these small beginnings, for the Lord rejoices to see the work begin.*

ZECHARIAH 4:10a

Delay no longer, my child. Determine this hour to bring forth your long-held dreams. This carefully conceived treasure wrapped in fine linen, preserved in the memory of your heart.

The creativity of hope concealed from eyes of others, but made known to me, your Father, years ago when we dreamed together the possibility. Bring to light, uncover the creative offering that will touch lives, save souls, and recast your future.

Behold! The oppressor who has sought to silence your voice and crush the light from this dream through circumstance of pain and loss. This oppressor, at long last is bound. Your fierce battles of war upon the plains of territorial prayer have released the angelic. The roar of the Lion sounded your advancement, step-by-determined-step, birthed this moment of triumph and deliverance.

Eagles of light, circle in the atmosphere of battle, their cry, Victor! Overcomer! The sound resonates and seals the conclusion. It is finished!

Today is your launch. Rise and unveil your efforts and new beginnings for I AM breathing life into your dreams once more. My hand of blessing is poised over your work. Trust that your labors of love for people, animals, and nature have been recorded in the scrolls of heaven. The records that reflect your faithful living, they now place a demand upon my power and move my heart.

Prosperity, open doors, provision are my blessings in this season. Unveil your hopes to the world and release your dreams with creative work. Observe, all to which you have labored in the secret place is now ready for the public. I bless your humble offerings.

I delight in small beginnings. It is my joy to imagine with you and reveal my love through your dreams.

 Father, thank you for dreaming with me. I step into this realm of creativity and dream aloud with you today. I am determined to bring the dreams you gave me into this world that you would be honored and glorified and to release your love to others. I step with humility and with boldness into this dream I've long held in my heart. I receive your provision to create all that this dream holds, here upon the earth. Thank you, Father, for lavishing love, provision, and your creative hand upon my life. In Jesus' name. AMEN

THE CLIMATE OF SHALOM

> *The Lord himself goes before you and will be with you; he will never leave you nor forsake you. Do not be afraid; do not be discouraged.*

DEUTERONOMY 31:8

In this world you will face fear, pain, struggles, trauma, and an abundance of difficulties. But, you the chosen one of God, be of great cheer, you are surrounded by the Shalom of heaven. Walk each day in supernatural, authentic joy and peace of the Kingdom! For I have overcome this world of struggle for you. I hold the Key of David and beckon. I open the gates of peace and you are welcomed.

Today surrender your questions of why. Give unto me your need for explanation. Place into my scarred hands your disappointment, offense, fear, failures, and broken dreams. Today, for this day, step into the climate of Shalom and truly live in my peace that surpasses all understanding. Receive my love that redeems your heart from the fears of the world. My perfect love casts out all fear, doubt, and strife.

It is your Father's good pleasure to give you the keys to the Kingdom. Step into Shalom and feel my love. My love and joy will empower you to love others with a full heart, free from fear and worry.

Hallelujah!!!!!

> *I have told you these things, so that in me*
> *you may have peace. In this world you*
> *will have trouble. But take heart! I*
> *have overcome the world.*
> *JOHN 16:33*

 Father God, today, I step into your perfect peace. I give you my need to know "why." I will stand on the faithfulness of your presence in my life. You said you will never leave me nor forsake me. This is where I choose to live today. I receive your blessings of perfect peace over my mind, heart, body, will, and emotions. I am covered by the blood of Jesus. I choose to walk in your love and truth. In Jesus' name. AMEN

DIVINE EXCHANGE

> *Come to me, all you who are weary and burdened, and I will give you rest. Take my yoke upon you and learn from me, for I am gentle and humble in heart, and you will find rest for your souls. For my yoke is easy and my burden is light.*
>
> *MATTHEW 11:28-30*

I AM the God of The Great Exchange.

I AM the giver of good gifts. This truth often appears as a paradox, a puzzle. My children refrain to seek the exchange out of ignorance or fear.

Beauty for ashes.

Blessing instead of curses.

Healing in place of disease.

Love over rejection.

Salvation over damnation.

The Divine Exchange. A holy encounter. A moment of intimacy.

A vulnerable surrender of wounding. The surrender of injustice. The place of trust into my hands of memories of painful betrayal, cruel childhoods, broken promises, failed expectations. A beautiful exchange of lost dreams.

My children cling to these places in their soul. They are nurtured, developed, and protected. But when these wounds are viewed in the Spirit, they appear gaping, seeping, and infected gashes that covertly bleed into other healthy areas of the mind, body, soul, and emotions.

Jesus, my Son, is the healer. His resurrection ushered in many gifts to mankind, (Ephesians 4:8). He willingly, lovingly, and with tenderhearted kindness brokers the Great Exchange.

My child don't delay your exchange. Offer to Jesus your ache, grief, and betrayals. Ask him for the exchange. Give him your pain and ask him for a new gift. Then walk with him this day and you will be free indeed. Ask him for your new dream today.

 Jesus, today I seek this divine exchange. Take my wounding, fear, and failures. Heal the places of pain in my soul, mind, and emotions. Pour out your healing over these areas and release the gifts that you have for me in their place. Thank you for the sacrifice you made that heals me and makes me whole through your love. In your name, Jesus, I pray. AMEN

RESPLENDENT GLORY

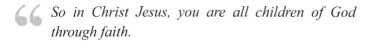

> *So in Christ Jesus, you are all children of God
> through faith.*
>
> *GALATIANS 3:24*

Why do my people struggle? Why do they experience setbacks in their faith?

A crisis of identity.

I have bestowed a profound gift upon my children. A Mantle, a garment of protection and a shield of strength. This coat is bound in leather and sealed with crimson. The forces of hell cannot forge against it nor penetrate the heart.

My children perish for lack of knowledge. They are unaware this mantle is available and waiting to be shouldered and worn into battle and throughout life. It's my free and unrestrained gift. I have created it uniquely for each one. It can never be stolen or thwarted. Its power is of military might and branded to move mountains.

When my children identify as mine and step into the wrap, they become complete, sealed in. Then perspectives change, truth and reality and circumstance are viewed and lived from eternity. It is the power of heaven come to earth to serve and to dwell in the promise (John10:10).

My children abandon their mantles in the dust, disheveled about their feet unaware. The evil one is pilfering their identity, their hope, and their aspirations.

Today, pray and declare that the children of the King will take up their God-given identity and walk in it. Thus, they shall see the goodness of the LORD in the land of the living.

They shall see my resplendent glory!

Pick up this mantle and walk in it! Hallelujah!

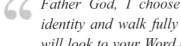 *Father God, I choose this hour to pick up my identity and walk fully in all that you say I am. I will look to your Word to define me. I will not look for affirmation and acceptance among the lies of the world. I seek your face, your purposes, and your will for my life. I choose this hour to live boldly as your child and reflect the love of Christ to those around me. In Jesus' name. AMEN*

6

EXPECTANT FAITH

> *The thief comes only to steal and kill and destroy; I have come that they may have life, and have it to the full.*
>
> *JOHN 10:10*

E xpect good things. Stop expecting bad.

For the plans I have for you are all good!

I came to give you hope and abundant life. Stop speaking the language of lack. Change your speech, change your understanding. I am not a God of barely enough. I am a God who performs exceedingly, abundantly more than you can ask or imagine.

At my right hand are blessings, forevermore. I have storehouses of treasures available for you, but you must believe and hope that it CAN BE possible.

Determine to take your eyes off yourself and place them back on ME. Stop being led and controlled by fear. Let your trust and confidence in ME be what leads you continually.

When you don't know what to do, talk to me. When you are afraid, call to me. I will comfort you and give you the confidence to move forward.

Don't expect to do this alone. You are NOT alone. I AM with you!!!

 Father God, I have moments of fear and doubt. I call out as you beckon me to step into your presence. Wrap confidence around me as a mantle. Let me speak your words of truth and goodness into my life covered by your love and goodness. Place into me the Spirit of Wisdom and Revelation, (Ephesians 1:17), to know your will for my life today. Let me hear you speak to me and walk with me out of fear and into hope of your grace, mercy, and love. In the name of my Savior, Jesus. AMEN

BREAKING THE SOUL TIES OF LIES

> *"The Lord bless him!" Naomi said to her daughter-in-law. "He has not stopped showing his kindness to the living and the dead." She added, "That man is our close relative; he is one of our guardian-redeemers."*

RUTH 2:20

The Hebrew word for guardian-redeemer is a legal term for one who has the obligation to redeem a relative in serious difficulty. (NIV notation)

I see the difficulty of earthly relationships that have held you bound in fear and insecurity, longing for any fragment of affection or affirmation. I understand your yearning to be loved and accepted by people that should be first to defend you, stand with you, and to love you unconditionally. I know your heart has felt the sting of rejection and the sadness of loss. I have heard your lament over what could have been.

I also know the deception the enemy has employed to ensnare those who hurt you with fear, envy, and hatefulness. Their soul has slipped away into self-preservation, lies of corruption.

Release them to me!

I stand as your Family Redeemer to break every unhealthy bond which holds your heart captive. I release you from the prison of false hope that one day they will love you. I free you from the ties and lies that have choked your emotions and held you captive seeking any morsel of love and attention. You are free this very hour from the pretense of affirmation that will never arrive.

Today, bless them. Release them in prayer to me. Receive my freedom and healing of your broken and wounded heart. I will take care of them.

Today, receive my love and friendship. Know that I wait with anticipation each morning for your eyelids to open, for you to wake so that I can pour out my affirmation and joy into your life. Let me affirm your soul with perfect love and wholeness.

You are my child. I adore you and you are perfect and amazing in every way!

 Father God, I surrender my disappointment, pain, and the expectation I have placed upon others. I ask you to take the pain and regrets of lost relationships and fill those empty spaces in my soul with your unfailing and perfect love and grace. Lord, do not let my heart grow bitter but lead me instead to live every day expectantly, listening to your voice and walking in your truth, love, and hope. And one day if those who have rejected me,

turn, and seek me out, I will open my arms in love through your transforming power. In Jesus' name. AMEN

RECEIVE MERCY AND GRACE

> *Let us then approach God's throne of grace with confidence, so that we may receive mercy and find grace to help us in our time of need.*

HEBREWS 4:16

Beloved child of God, I extend my invitation to approach. Come boldly to my Throne of Grace for I have listened as you have travailed in prayerful petition. I discern your whispers of hope for this season of trouble that contemplates you with grim oppression. The dreams you long ago surrendered under the crushing of life circumstances.

Hear me now my beloved child, I AM breathing upon them in this season. I AM releasing grace from heaven in this hour. Approach my Throne, you are welcome here.

Refuse to be deceived by your experience or understanding. Your past and present are mine to heal and reframe through lenses of love in a twinkling of an eye. You are not disqualified, incapacitated, nor deemed unable or unworthy to receive my fullness.

I beckon your approach and then perceive the grace at my right hand and my mercy that rushes into your life with an answer to your questions and fear. I have more than enough wisdom and provision for your every need and unending love to sooth your woundedness. Do not fear. Do not doubt. All of heaven awaits for your voice to be heard.

Come near! My scepter of love is extended in a broad greeting. Come unto me and find rest. Come unto me and receive, come in and know my perfect love that casts out all fear.

 Father, I bring my broken and lost dreams and place them before your Throne. I will step into your grace and receive new hope, mercy, and your breath upon my life. Speak to me of your wisdom that I will make choices which lead to the highest and best life. AMEN

YOU HAVE EVERYTHING

> *His divine power has given us everything we need for a godly life through our knowledge of him who called us by his own glory and goodness.*

2 PETER 1:3

My child, have you finally grown weary? Is the cloak of frustration that covers your soul consuming your energies? Are the bonds of darkness—worry, unrest, anxiety—blotting out your brilliance, intellect, and power?

I look upon your heart and perceive your questions. Be assured, I am intently listening as you pray. Yet, my sweet child, bend your knee and pray differently.

Your prayers and petitions are scrambling for a hasty resolution to your current struggle and pain. But, alas, haste offers merely a temporary relief while closure remains aloof and distant. I long to place into your life a permanent healing, a remedy of such magnitude that never again will you struggle with this preponderance of ache.

Seek not simplicity of answers.

Seek revelation.

Seek my heart.

Turn the hours of petition-prayers into plunging prayer. Ask to enter in. Seek to be welcomed into depths of perfection. Jump off the cliff of mundane and safe footing, swim through the seas of love, grace, mercy. Touch the center of my heart. Worship in expectant peace. Rest in me.

Peace resides within revelation of my realm, providing every resolution to every problem of mankind.

Revelation unlocks wisdom. Request wisdom and I will send her to you, laden with scrolls of decree for your future. Revelation downloads transport simplicity of design to complicated challenges, impossible relationships, and evil assignments. Revelation is a realm of hope. It is joy personified in delight as resolutions arrive. It is all you need. Revelation is your power on earth, my child.

Seek revelation from my heart. Pray with greater understanding.

Behold!

The angelic are summoned. Warriors of God arrive. Give a SHOUT! Hallelujah! Strategies and blueprints from heaven unfold within your mind.

The mere answers you are seeking are swallowed up in GLORY as my revelation, purposes, love, and power are displayed through your life.

This day turn to revelation prayer. The move of God in your life will bring the awareness of me to others. Arise and take this world for the Kingdom of The Most High!

Father, I surrender to you my scrambling prayers. I know that you are good and have good things for my life. I ask for your perfect peace to rest upon me. Move in my life to resolve the circumstances that have created fear and worry. I ask for your revelation and I choose today to rest in you. In Jesus' name. AMEN

CONVERSATIONS WITH THE FATHER

> *He has saved us and called us to a holy life—not because of anything we have done but because of his own purpose and grace. This grace was given us in Christ Jesus before the beginning of time.*

2 TIMOTHY 1:9

I see the difficulty of earthly relationships that have held you bound, my child, yet you do not perceive all the goodness that surrounds you. Goodness is everywhere, in pockets of unrecognized love that is passed, person to person, good deed to good deed. Goodness is beheld in my love, manifesting in endless rounds of beauty in nature, hope in the human heart, provision, and creativity.

The sons of perdition work through deception to infiltrate goodness and plant seeds of hopelessness, confusion, sorrow, and despair.

But as a child of mine, you are fully equipped to destroy the works of the enemy. My child, step outside on this dazzling morning. What do you see?

Ponder the brilliant depths of the sunrise sky, evergreen trees with bristle cones of perfection and anointed with a divine aroma. Focus on the whistle of the birds; they are singing worship in an unrehearsed symphony.

Yes, my beloved child, every dawning of the day I listen as they fulfill their divine calling and fill the air with sound. It is the same when you pray. Melodies of love pierce my heart. Life is all about thriving, singing, creating. The natural world is a reflection of beauty and hope of the Kingdom, eternal.

My child, now consider the human mind. Its capacity remains woefully untapped by most. It remains a mystery to science, complex, brilliant, creative, powerful. And the human body is a creation of vast and varying systems complete in detail and function. Ah, my child, the spirit! The Spirit of God that dwells in the body. The spirit, my child, is where all things converge—intellect, wisdom, revelation, peace, divine health, power, authority…. Dominion.

I have already given you all you need for life and Godliness (2 Peter 1:3). It's in the Spirit. For your words are spirit and they are life (John 6:63). When you turn your pursuits away from the deceiver to fully focus upon my love, my nature, my purposes, and plans… Focus upon me and your spirit becomes fully alive. Within your spirit unfolds the wisdom of my power. And my power realigns your DNA to holiness and creates the Kingdom of God within. From within flows outwardly, rivers of living water that heals the ugly, repairs destruction, and redirects the difficult issues of life (John 7:37-38).

This is the truth, seek ye the Kingdom of God and all these things shall be added unto you. Pursue me and perceive. You SHALL see the goodness of the Lord in the land of the living.

My child, take me with you wherever you go today, and I shall reveal my glory in the ordinary and in the divine. All my love, your Father.

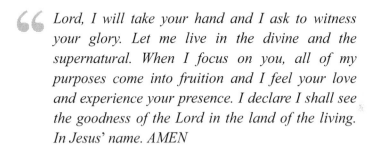

Lord, I will take your hand and I ask to witness your glory. Let me live in the divine and the supernatural. When I focus on you, all of my purposes come into fruition and I feel your love and experience your presence. I declare I shall see the goodness of the Lord in the land of the living. In Jesus' name. AMEN

WRITERS AND JOURNALISTS...WRITE

> Beautiful words stir my heart. I will recite a lovely poem about the king, for my tongue is like the pen of a skillful poet.

PSALM 45:1

The time is at hand to publish my deeds among the nations. Do NOT delay. I have called you to be my writing quill. I have placed a divine and holy mandate upon your hand.

Share your story.

Record the testimony.

Make the words immortal. There is a great power released by the testimony of my people and your story impacts lives, transforms hearts, and brings honor to my name.

The enemy has risen against my creatives. Stolen is the poetry and prose, the passion, the sacred words of my heart. He has planted the tares among the wheat—barbs of disappointment, rejection, and uncertainty... fear. The flood of his lies and assignment of disasters which are aimed at my scribes.... IT IS OVER!

I speak a word that my writers are ARISING with words of life, healing, truth, and hope. I am raising a Standard over my people. A banner of protection and encouragement. This banner of heaven over my scribes and journalists shouts, DO NOT DELAY! I am dispatching angels with quill and scroll. They are being sent to my writers and journalists. Lean in and listen, learn, and record. Write of my faithfulness, my healing, deliverance. Pen about my joy and of my merciful love.

Write of my Son.

Bring my hope to the people.

Your assignment is love.

Your assignment is the pen.

Your time is now!

 Father, I am your scribe and my pen is poised, ready. I will take down the words you provide and make them known among the people. I will record your words of joy, faithfulness, healing, hope, and mercy. Thank you, Father, that you chose me to be one who records the reality of your presence in this world. I will not delay to release your word those who need to know your fathomless love and goodness. In Jesus' name. AMEN

12

HOPE IS A SUBSTANCE

> *Praise the Lord, my soul; all my inmost being, praise his holy name. Praise the Lord, my soul, and forget not all his benefits— who forgives all your sins and heals all your diseases, who redeems your life from the pit and crowns you with love and compassion, who satisfies your desires with good things so that your youth is renewed like the eagle's.*

PSALM 103:1-5

I know the challenges of your life. I recognize the struggles in your home. I know that you often feel alone fighting for decency and godliness for yourself and your family. In the night hours, I am sitting next to you as the tears trail your cheek. I am holding your hand, my child.

I recognize the blows come in words which tear at your very soul. Disappointment tells you it's not worth the effort and whispers lies that are convincing you to admit defeat. I see your torment.

But today, I want you to know deep in your soul, I've been by your side every minute. You have a great hope. Your hope isn't just a wish or a thought that perhaps something will change. Your hope is alive and filled with truth that something will be better tomorrow.

HOPE in the Kingdom is a substance that is powerful. It is a word that when wielded in faith decimates the strongholds of argu-ment. It silences the defeat of unchanged lives and hearts. Hope is the greatest gift given to my children on earth.

When you lift words of prayer, with hope, this is the activation of powerful faith. I've blessed you with life and new beginnings. As believers, each morning that you arise it's your choice to step into a new life, new hope, and redemption of past lies, sins, and failures.

This is real hope. You have promises filled with real power. Truth that brings steadfastness and love that rearranges the impossible.

I know you feel weary. Bring your battle scars to me in the morning and I WILL HEAL THEM. In their place, I bestow medals of honor. They seal up the wounds and release power into your circumstances.

You are an overcomer. Let me remind you of this truth. You overcome the arrows of the enemy and you release light and truth. Your home and family are what the enemy wants to destroy more than anything else. Arise and fight, serve and pray for your family, GREAT IS YOUR REWARD. Each day you continue in hope releases a power to support and angels are set on assignment to walk with you.

Walk it out. Pray the torment stops this hour. Forbid the tormentor from speaking lies to you, your spouse, and children.

Pray the Holy Spirit into your home and into the hearts of those you love.

And hear me now.... I AM THERE WITH YOU. I will not let you fail. The fire rages about you, but what you are gaining in knowledge and experience is priceless.

When you are doubting or feeling defeated, open my Word. Read the promises from the Gospels aloud to yourself. Tell your soul, as David told his soul, these are my promises and I want every one of them for myself and my family. In Jesus' name.

Hope is your life. It is the substance that will carry you home and into the gates of the Kingdom. You will enter in with great cele-bration and adorned with badges of honor because you chose hope in the dark and you saw it come alive in the passing of the years.

I adore you. And I leave you this promise to stand upon today: I will never leave you nor forsake you.

The Lord, God, Almighty

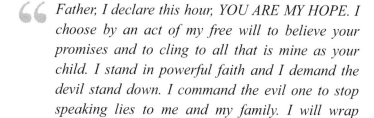

Father, I declare this hour, YOU ARE MY HOPE. I choose by an act of my free will to believe your promises and to cling to all that is mine as your child. I stand in powerful faith and I demand the devil stand down. I command the evil one to stop speaking lies to me and my family. I will wrap myself in your promises and one day step into heaven escorted by faith, hope, and love. AMEN

13

CLARITY OF VISION

> *Trust in the Lord with all your heart and lean not on your own understanding; in all your ways submit to him, and he will make your paths straight.*

PROVERBS 3:5-6

In this season I AM releasing clarity of vision.

Your steadfast faith and persistent prayers, seeking wisdom and divine understanding, now bear the full weight upon the Scales of Righteousness in my House. You have restrained your habitual responses thereby through determined submission, brought your confusion and lack of understanding before me. You did not tread in the valley of human explanation of limited view.

Instead, your petitions with thanksgiving arrive before me in long tendrils of swirling mist intertwined with words claiming my wisdom over your questions. Prayers drawing a demand on the grace and peace of heaven, that rest heavy upon your heart.

This is the day that all of heaven gathers. The tipping of the Kingdom scales, poised, ready, and prepared upon my command. Wisdom accompanied by knowledge and faith rush forth with the angel, Grace, released and descending. The shout echoes through the eons. Go to my children. Wisdom speaks decrees which shatter the bite of bitterness. Angels of action, receive your assignment. Go forth with treasuries, maps, blueprints, strategies, ointments of healing, and oils of peace, joy, and righteousness.

The scales are tipping, rushing the blessings of God along with the fire of heaven which destroys the enemy of the Crown.

Redemption! The shouts reverberate through the ancient halls, down the ladder to the people. The King of Glory is releasing heaven's response to the determined intercession of the people. Well done, intercessors. Well done, my child. Your faithful stewardship of your thought life, prayers, and restraint availed lavishness in the season of Kingdom advancement.

Receive my wisdom, grace, and mercy. Receive my vindication, receive the answers to your petitions, and then arise into the new assignment of glory that will delight your heart and fill your soul.

 Father, in the name of Jesus, I receive this word of justice. I am humbled that my prayers have tipped the scales in heaven. I await with an open spirit to receive the blessings of abundance you have for me and all that I steward. I give you thanks and I worship your name, Yahweh. I praise you and declare you are my Lord and my God. AMEN

14

RELEASE, RESTORATION AND FREEDOM

> *Ask and it will be given to you; seek and you will find; knock and the door will be opened to you. For everyone who asks receives; the one who seeks finds; and to the one who knocks, the door will be opened.*

MATTHEW 7:7-8

It is not a time for idle chitchat.

It's not a time for monotone prayer.

This is a quickly passing season of breakthrough and you are poised on the edge to step in and receive the anointing stored up for you.

This is the time for travailing prayer. War in your words for your breakthrough. Pray aloud your healing. Seek and ye shall find. Knock and it will be opened unto you. Knock and I will open the door. I stand before you. Knock and I will open the door that you may enter into my peace, health, restoration, and freedom.

Enter into my joy!

Hallelujah, AMEN!

 Father, in the name of Jesus I come before you and I speak this verse in Matthew back to you in faith: Ask and it will be given to you; seek and you will find; knock and the door will be opened to you. For everyone who asks receives; the one who seeks finds; and to the one who knocks, the door will be opened.

I believe in your Word and I stand at the door and knock. I boldly open the door and approach your throne of grace and present my requests to you. Bring the restoration of all the enemy has stolen from my relationships, my finances, my health, and every other area of my life. I seek the Kingdom with a full and hungry heart. I believe you move upon my petitions and I stand in faith to receive your goodness and blessing today. In Jesus' name, I make this petition. AMEN

15

DEFEATING CONFUSION

> *Peace I leave with you; my peace I give you. I do not give to you as the world gives. Do not let your hearts be troubled and do not be afraid.*

JOHN 14:27

A great spirit of confusion has come upon the land. Its assignment is division, worry, and paralysis. I perceive the mind of my people spinning, whirring away, calculating every possible outcome to overwhelming circumstances. This confusion breeds indecision, which holds minds and lives captive. The perpetual, ever-spinning circle of this prison feels as though it will never end.

But I hear the LORD!

He comes in like a flood against this spinning, black whirlwind with his STANDARD raised high.

SILENCE – PEACE – He speaks!

The demons tremble. Calm is released. Broken are the chains of paralysis. Shattered are the teeth of addiction. Maimed and motionless are the spirits of death, mental illness, and hopelessness.

The Father's love has arrived! His Son, Jesus, has paid the price. Freedom, restoration, a sound mind ride in with him on a white horse. The land, our homes, our minds, and our lives are rescued. Peace, joy, and righteousness have come. The Kingdom has come.

AT LAST. HALLELUJAH!

> *So shall they fear The name of the Lord*
> *from the west, And His glory from the*
> *rising of the sun; When the enemy*
> *comes in like a flood, The Spirit of the*
> *Lord will lift up a standard against*
> *him.*
> *ISAIAH 59:19*

 Jesus, in your name I stand against confusion and will not allow it to speak into my life circumstances. I stand upon your blood covenant and in faith. I will look to your truth to guide me and to be my strength and my peace. AMEN

16

STEADFAST FAITH

66 *When you hear them sound a long blast on the trumpets, have the whole army give a loud shout; then the wall of the city will collapse and the army will go up, everyone straight in.*

JOSHUA 6:5

In the current hour I sense a monstrous assault against identity. The whispers of lies of unworthiness, left out, forgotten, not good enough, not strong enough, funny, flirty and, and, and…. There is an effort right now by the enemy to undo the difficult efforts made toward healing and wholeness.

THAT STOPS NOW!

I am not unaware of your schemes, evil. And now hear me echo the roar from heaven. In the name of Jesus, I SHOUT, "SILENCE!" I choose to reject lies I have fought to overcome and remain STEADFAST in the truth.

I AM AN EMPOWERED CHILD OF GOD!

Perseverance is my creed. Love, my mission. Compassion, my strength. Courage, my shield and hope, my lifestyle. I choose life. I choose to walk in truth. I choose Jesus.

Amen!

 Jesus, this very hour grant me supernatural discernment to recognize the subtle lies of evil. Create in me your passion that took you to the Cross that I would stand in steadfast faith. I make this declaration today; I am an empowered child of God. My mission is clear, and I will not waver off the path of the victorious in Christ. I fight for my wholeness and that of my family. I stand against injustice and for the liberty of the captives held by the devil. I shout your name, JESUS. You are truth and all that I will ever need. In your mighty name, Jesus. AMEN

17

LISTEN TO THE SPIRIT OF WISDOM

 Weeping may endure for a night, but joy cometh in the morning.

PSALM 30:5b

Who among my people will incline an ear? Who is listening to the wisdom of the Spirit? The pressure of this sifting, the building of the forces of strife, bear down. The character of my people, forged in the flames of contention and opposition as hell rages against them, roaring, reaching a crescendo.

Tears. The many tears are captured by angelic hosts in bottles of remembrance. They are sealed, each one, in the storerooms of heaven. Labeled with tender care and meaning—loss, infirmity, poverty, addiction, death. Testimonies upon the shelves. Each an assignment of hell determined with an assail of weeping and destruction of my children.

The tears of the Bride sealed, recorded, and waiting, each for the redemption and restoration that looms and quickly draws nigh. Each demands the recompense of the Ancient One.

This shall surely happen! The shout from heaven reverberates across time and space.

Perceive the fires which accomplish the burning away of the dross throughout the months ahead. This refining then turns the page to the season of surrender as the old life of defeat marches to its close. Many perceived losses and concluded assignments draw down to finality and closure.

Do you not perceive it, my child? Are you unaware that my hand is moving to release you into the new?

The decrees of life bursts forth, ALL THINGS NEW! The Kingdom of God releases the angelic multitude, wings of determined flight and missions, certain. Millions of heavenly scrolls arrive with new assignments. The arrival is accompanied with provision for completion. Works of healing, salvation of the nations, teachings, preaching, creative blueprints of discovery. Each an intimate design to release my love, joy, peace in increasing measure.

My child, open your spirit. Take an account of the details in your current season that are drawing down to culmination. Much of what you grip in a stronghold and fear of loss is determined to hinder. Let go, for my purpose must be fulfilled in your life and the lives of others.

There is pain, sorrow, not by my hand, but by my enemy. Yet, through my compassion I will close the sorrowful season.

Yea, however!

The trumpet blast of **RENEWAL** decrees the end! The birth of new life, new anointings, exceptional possibilities and increase into your future and beyond. Remain steadfast. Your awareness now, is the key titled, Overcomer. It unlocks the treasuries of heaven. Behold the tears of yesterday are redeemed in new adventure and assignments and the enemy will repay, times seven, all that was lost and taken.

Prayer, faith, and conviction are your courage to press through.

I delight to give you the Kingdom. Thou art being prepared in this season for the weighty glory to rest upon you with increased measure.

Hallelujah. AMEN!

 Father, my spirit resonates under this passionate decree of a new season. I stand in full faith that the season of testing has reached its zenith and it is now drawing down to a close. I give you my tears and even my questions. I know in this new season the reason and the answers will arrive out of your goodness and love. I believe you have goodness for me and I speak it into this new season and the months ahead. In my Jesus' name. AMEN

18

BREAKING CHAINS OF SHAME

> *For the kingdom of God is not a matter of eating and drinking, but of righteousness, peace and joy in the Holy Spirit.*

ROMANS 14:17

Shame is a wicked master. It grips the hearts and minds of my children and draws them away from me and turns them inward. It creeps upon many and winds cruel fetters of bondage around their hopes and future.

My child, my beloved, you are not a mistake. You are NOT what you did or what has happened to you. You are fun and fantastic. You are destined for good things. You are created to dream and experience abundance, power, fullness, and delight. Your place in the Kingdom is love, power, and a sound mind.

I banish the spirit of shame from your life.

Rise up, my child, with boldness.

Rise up, beloved, without fear.

Rise up, my Kingdom Warrior, and take your place as heir with Christ. I shatter the chains of shame and bestow upon you regal peace, joy, and righteousness. Righteousness is life without guilt, free from shame and all condemnation.

It is said of thee: Well done, good and faithful servant.

 Father, I'm choosing today to believe your Word about who I am and whose I am. I am a child who is free from the accusations of the devil. I am absolved of the condemning words of my childhood. I step out of the guilt and blame game to walk in the freedom that was purchased at the Cross. Reveal where shame hides within and walk with me into divine healing to be truly free to love without limits. In Christ's name and by his blood. AMEN

19

MORNINGS WITH FATHER

> *May you be blessed by the Lord, the Maker of heaven and earth. The highest heavens belong to the Lord, but the earth he has given to mankind.*

PSALM 115:15-16

G ood morning, Father of unending love and grace. Your hands are filled with every manner of blessing. Your love radiates in the colors of nature, the pastels of the olive leaves, the brilliant bridal white and the delicate scent of a Gardenia blossom. All of nature cheers your splendor and the loyalty of your goodness. We behold your radiance with a mere glance into the sapphire of the morning firmament. We perceive as you surround us with commonplace miracles such as a bumble bee upon its morning pursuit as well as finches flitting among the branches or the intricacies of a newly spun web. Our soul gate perceives your grace, mercy, and your attributes which are on continual display in everyday moments in the world of nature.

Today, Father, bring forth these reflections of your splendor. Prompt me to display your attributes back into this world through a kind word to a stranger, a hug for the lonely, and healing for the brokenhearted. Let me speak a word of life from the WORD OF LIFE to a hurting soul!

 Abba, Father, my soul is made whole when I take in the majesty of your creation in the natural world. Compel my heart to explore creation and allow what I behold to change me. Let your love flow through me that I will be a voice to others to bring your healing to a hurting and broken soul. I ask this in Jesus' name. AMEN

WELCOME TO MY TABLE OF THANKS

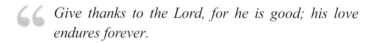

> *Give thanks to the Lord, for he is good; his love endures forever.*

PSALM 118:1

Cease your struggle and worry. Put away the frantic demands upon your time and energy. Bow low, shrug off the burdens, laden with discord, competition, and foolish striving. In this season, I welcome you to my Table.

Washed and prepared, anointed with the oil of heaven, I beckon you to receive the plates of bounty I've set before you. This holy encounter, an invitation from the King of Glory.

Be seated, as the meal is about to ensue, a sacred experience. As you receive to becoming full, you will be emptied.

The invitation is given. Will you accept and participate in the meal of the holy and the divine?

The silver stems of the placements gleam, reflecting a myriad of color. The golden table setting, shimmers, as alive. The Table of

Honor is readied before you, awaiting the service of bounty of the Kingdom.

The courses prepared, angelic service at hand. The anticipation of your delight, twinkles in their lavender eyes as they behold your countenance. They pause with understanding as the power of this partaking is unlike any other.

Child, raise your chalice, a tribute to your courage in the face of fear. An honor of a lifetime of treading through the battles and landmines of life. The applause of heaven breaks forth.

My child, I approve of your smile as the delicacies arrive prepared specifically for you.

This is the Banquet of the Divine. Surrender on this day, a lifetime of starvation and devastation, and choose the better.

Fill your plate with peace and cast-off worry.

A slice of pure joy served before you, release the constraint of religion.

A portion of gladness and your broken heart is mended.

One helping of faithfulness conveys in a lifetime of confidence.

Add to your plate, my provision, as lack then must depart.

A dash of protection and fear is surrendered.

Taste the power of my presence. Fear is banished into the darkness.

The angels dance about the table as your meal proceeds, their joy unrestrained. The transformation occurring at the Table of Grace brings all of heaven to assembly in praise.

My beloved child, welcome to the Kingdom Thanksgiving dinner.

You are my welcomed family. On this day receive the bounty I have waiting for you. Use the keys I've provided through my Word. Unlock the treasuries, the storehouses, the healing rooms of the Kingdom. Turn the Key of Love, release the latch through thankful living, raise the handle of faith to walk into the fullness of my Kingdom.

Welcome to the Table of the Divine.

 My heavenly Father, I offer up my thanksgiving for this beautiful table prepared in my honor. I bestow unto you, Lord, honor, worship, and humble thankfulness for how you provide for me each and every day. Thank you for your goodness, bounty, and your welcome at this table of the Divine. AMEN

21

ALL THINGS POSSIBLE

  Very truly I tell you, whoever believes in me will do the works I have been doing, and they will do even greater things than these, because I am going to the Father. And I will do whatever you ask in my name, so that the Father may be glorified in the Son. You may ask me for anything in my name, and I will do it.

JOHN 12:12-14

Nothing is impossible!

Jesus is the gate to open the possible. Become participants in the fantastic and witness the impractical unfold before your very eyes.

I am the gate; whoever enters through me will be saved. They will come in and go out and find pasture (John 10:9).

The enemy has distorted and hidden the path to the gate—the abundant life. His lies of fear and misunderstanding are now revealed and laid bare. We crush every pretension and lie of deception under our feet.

Jesus said, I am the gate. He is the gate to possibilities, extremes, and implausible adventures.

It's your turn!!!

The path illuminated in the love of Jesus, now is revealed. Throw wide the gate of "all things possible." Let the love of God speak to you every day. Participate with angels. The supernatural is our inheritance, it is our birthright! Open up, child of God, and ask!

Ask, and it will be given to you; seek, and you will find; knock, and it will be opened to you (Matthew 7:7).

Open the gate and let the adventures begin.

 Jesus, teach me to believe and expect the impossible. Stir up within me a fierce faith and boldness that I will dream, pray, and then trust expectantly for you to bring me through the impossible circumstances to prove your faithfulness, love, and power. Do not let the enemy steal my desires and hopes, but I ask you to rouse them to life this very hour. Allow me to catch glimpses of what you have prepared for me to do and all you desire for me to become. Grant me Joshua courage to step into the plans of heaven and be a firebrand for the Kingdom of Yahweh. In your powerful name, Jesus. AMEN

22

HIDDEN TREASURES

> " *I will give you hidden treasures, riches stored in secret places, so that you may know that I am the LORD, the God of Israel, who summons you by name.*

ISAIAH 45:3

I have hidden treasures all around your day.

My hand of love placed each one, a divine intersection. A memorial stone, a remembrance of who you are and whose you are. Your faithfulness and devotion to me, acts of love and obedience, each recorded in the books. Your name scrolled, authored within the Lamb's Book of Life. Your name shimmers of brilliant gold, crimson, and silver, and is alive and ever before me.

I behold, as you tarry in the early morning hours before the light of dawn, leaning into my Word. Your heart fully open to receive my wisdom, grace, and instruction. The years of quiet contemplation have gathered a mighty army of angelic hosts about you.

And in this hour, you dispatch with commands, initiating the work of the Kingdom for the day.

You are my BELOVED! You are alive in me and I in you. Look all around you. See the hidden treasures awaiting your discovery and delight. Love notes penned to affirm, inspire, and speak of my heart.

My beloved child, in your relentless pursuit, you have acquired the ways of the Kingdom. You have chosen the narrow road and upon this path I've placed the fantastic. Resources of healing, angelic, signs, and wonders.

Step in today and behold. It is my great pleasure to give you these hidden treasures of the Kingdom!

 Father, thank you for revealing your heart to me. Today lead me share your love with those around me. In Jesus' name. AMEN

YOUR FREEDOM DAY

> O Lord, I have so many enemies; so many are against me. So many are saying, "God will never rescue him! But you, O Lord, are a shield around me; you are my glory, the one who holds my head high."

PSALM 3:1-3

Deeply, secretly, within your heart reside saved up words; disappointment, forgotten, unrealized, sidelined. The words couple with your fading dreams, lost hopes, and unfulfilled emotions. My child, your efforts to surrender thorns in your spirit, when remembered, sting afresh; the words prick, they bleed, and you have withstood the pain through your valiant faith.

I stood near, listening as your whispered prayers of surrender and forgiveness, seeking resolution. Yet, deep within the longing of your soul, they remain. They speak at night into the silence, I matter. I hurt. I remain.

I perceive the reluctance to stare at the truth, but in your spirit, you are disappointed in me. Unvoiced, but loud in the spiritual, are whispers that I could have intervened in the messes of your life. The outcome would have been different, should have been different.

Ah, my child, but I was.

What you cannot observe in the limited perspectives of earthly life is that I AM in the circumstances. I stood by your side, even lifting you at times out of mortal danger, financial disaster, devastating tragedy, and further loss. My child, I AM powerfully capable. I AM bearing each of your disappointments. Bring your disappointments and confusion out of the festering cavern of your heart. Expose your pain to the light.

Share with me. Forgive others, forgive yourself. Forgive even me if that is your need. I will bear your grief, anger, confusion, and fears. Surrender it all.

And in time, I promise you I will restore or replace what was taken, lost, and stolen. Lasting peace and understanding will arrive, and peace will cover and heal your pain.

The hurts of today are a promise for tomorrow. I have new destinies for you, my child, better than the old. Assignments of adventure, astonishing accomplishments, gifts and surprises, a life of divine direction, that overflows with fulfillment, peace, joy, and my goodness.

I AM capable and willing to walk you through your disappointments. Trust, one brick at a time, as you build trust in me. I trust you. Trust me in one circumstance, one decision by faith. One-by-one we are building the foundation of an authentic, powerful, and happy life.

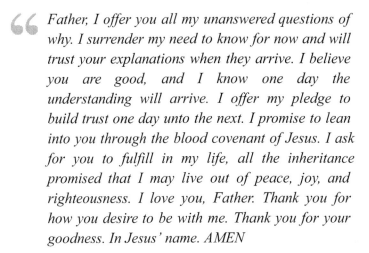

Father, I offer you all my unanswered questions of why. I surrender my need to know for now and will trust your explanations when they arrive. I believe you are good, and I know one day the understanding will arrive. I offer my pledge to build trust one day unto the next. I promise to lean into you through the blood covenant of Jesus. I ask for you to fulfill in my life, all the inheritance promised that I may live out of peace, joy, and righteousness. I love you, Father. Thank you for how you desire to be with me. Thank you for your goodness. In Jesus' name. AMEN

THE VOICE OF HOPE

> *And there were shepherds living out in the fields nearby, keeping watch over their flocks at night. An angel of the Lord appeared to them, and the glory of the Lord shone around them, and they were terrified. But the angel said to them, "Do not be afraid. I bring you good news that will cause great joy for all the people. Today in the town of David a Savior has been born to you; he is the Messiah, the Lord. This will be a sign to you: You will find a baby wrapped in cloths and lying in a manger."*

LUKE 2:8-12

Years of antiquity, long since passed, in a singular moment of time, a Prince was born. Conceived in holiness, brought forth and swaddled in lowliness. His name declared in the heavens with shouts of wonder, from the angels on High. The pride of his Father.

His name, Emmanuel—God with us.

This humble child, a gift to the multitudes who toil in bitterness and strife. The years of his youth, his stature increased as love and wisdom grew, gaining favor with God and mankind. His voice, a ministry of kindness, mercy, repentance, and forgiveness, releasing the people to hope once again, to believe and witness the power of a good Father.

Raised as an example to follow. His message was clear:

- Peace silences confusion and fear.
- Truth frees the mind from anxiety, depression, addiction, and trauma.
- Joy restores hope and creativity.
- Righteous conquers illness.
- Forgiveness heals the heart, mind, and soul.
- Love defeats hate.

This baby born and placed in a trough made for animals, grown, then hung on a tree. Cursed with the sins of all humanity, now forgiven. The power of heaven lights the sky. Flashes of victory and out of death he rises in blazing glory. The world now redeemed. Time split in two. Miracles and healing declared for earth.

In centuries long past, he was born the lowliest of Kings. Now raised to life, he reigns unmatched, to restore our hope, heal hearts, establish health, and defeat darkness.

He is:

The King of Kings

Lion of Judah

Bright and Morning Star

Prince of Peace

Emmanuel

He is Jesus.

Come to me, all you who are weary and burdened, and I will give you rest (Matthew 11:28).

 Jesus, you are my hope and my future. Thank you for your humble beginnings and your victory at the cross. I ask you to live within my heart and rule in my life. I ask you to forgive my failures and offenses and I choose to forgive others. Today, I receive the gift of eternal life. I am a new creation and receive salvation through the Holy Spirit. In your name, Jesus. AMEN

RELEASE THE CAPTIVES

> *He will wipe every tear from their eyes, and there*
> *will be no more death or sorrow or crying or pain.*
> *All these things are gone forever.*

REVELATION 21:4

There are many of my children who have languished in this end-time season, locked away as a prisoner of war, restrained in the enemy's camp. The barbed wire of disillusionment and abandonment have gouged the souls of humanity, leaving them bleeding and scared. This extended, grueling season of illness, scarcity, fear, and persecution has devastated their very soul. They are casualties of war, left abandoned on the plains of a bitter battlefield. Whispers of finality through betrayal, hopelessness, apathy, and fear are the lies that fortify their restraints.

These are my beloved children who loved me and once believed in my truths and Kingdom. But the blows of darkness birthed perceived falsehoods, speaking the decisive lie that I remained aloof and unaware of their sufferings. They turned toward the lies that my sovereign hand somehow allowed the brokenness and tears to overwhelm their faith and trust.

From my Throne, my voice thunders with peeling cracks of raw emotion and booming love.

IT IS NOT SO!

My love and power are always enough to liberate every soul.

You keep track of all my sorrows. You have collected all my tears in your bottle. You have recorded each one in your book (Psalm 56:8).

I have wept with you as I collected every tear as a token of restitution that is due. I have stored each droplet that cries out for vindication of all that the evil one has stolen.

Today, my children who are beset by bitterness and strife, determine your heart to trust me again. Pray. Speak to me once more, for I never left you alone. People may have failed you, left you devastated, lost in rejection, but I stand for you. I am your hope, redemption, your healing, life, and I have every answer to your questions. I AM your place of refuge.

Delay not another moment. Release your heart to me. I'm a moment away. Your faith and my love are your healing script. Pray without ceasing and never give up.

 Father, the battle has been intense, and I face moments of confusion when I feel as though you are far away. I know that in the fire it's difficult to perceive what your hand is preparing, touching, and redeeming. Place within me a steadfast faith to trust the process, even in the pain. Place within me the truth that I will understand in the future as that is your heart to reveal the answers to my questions.

Father, today I decree again my unwavering faith and my dedication to you and your Kingdom. Release answers today and show me throughout the day how you are imparting care and love over my life. In Jesus' name. AMEN

SCEPTER OF LOVE

> Let us then approach God's throne of grace with confidence, so that we may receive mercy and find grace to help us in our time of need.

HEBREWS 4:16

M y child, I invite you to approach boldly my Throne of Grace. For I have listened as you have prayed, and I discern your whispers of hope.

Your desires, long ago surrendered, under the crushing of life's disappointment and storms. But approach as I am breathing upon them with multifaceted grace in this hour. Come to my throne, you are welcomed here.

Do not be deterred by your experience or understanding. Your past and present belong to me to be redeemed and changed in a twinkling of an eye. You are not disqualified, incapacitated, nor unworthy to receive my fullness. I become your present. Grace and mercy stand ready and waiting to rush into your life with answers and the peace you seek, provision for your need, and love to soothe each wound of your soul.

Do not fear. Do not doubt. All of heaven waits for your voice to be heard. Approach, as my scepter of love is extended in broad welcome.

Come unto me and you shall find rest.

Child of the King, approach my Throne of Grace and receive mercy in your time of need.

 Lord, I step out of fear and come with a bold faith. I step before you with my hands full with the concerns of my life. I hold before you my fears, doubts, and struggles. I seek your kindness and I believe, by faith, that you have mercy and grace to meet each need. I believe that today I will begin to perceive your divine wisdom and the answers to my questions, fears, and struggles. Thank you, Father, that you love me, and thank you that I am welcomed in your presence. AMEN

27

PEACE IN THE SECRET PLACE

> *Fear not, for I am with you; Be not dismayed, for I am your God. I will strengthen you, Yes, I will help you, I will uphold you with my righteous right hand.*

ISAIAH 41:10

My child, ask of me your questions. Dare, through childlike innocence, to bring before me your confusion and doubts. Express your frustration and don't conceal the disappointment that is hidden in the cleft of your heart. Bring forward the pain of delay and reveal it to The Light.

Ask me of the challenging uncertainties you face and the why of it all. Ask the questions you dared not speak. Seek the answers with honesty and diligence. Compare your ponderings to my Word. Ask yourself, "Why isn't my life aligning to the truth that is revealed in the Word?" Ask then, "What lie am I believing about myself or God?"

The lie of delay is a device of my enemy and NOT of my hand. Pain is the enemy's tool to sideline you from life, to isolate, and release hopelessness. Fear is the weapon of choice of the evil realm to steal your voice, purpose, decimate your faith, and destroy your family.

It is my great pleasure to reveal the truth of your circumstances. I am a good Father. Delay, pain, confusion, fear—these are NOT of my Kingdom. These are devices of evil.

Today, I implore you, my child, bring me your unanswered questions. Carry to me the disappointment of lost hopes, broken relationships, and your unanswered pain. Enter into the secret place and release the questions, cloaked in a lie.

Seek the truth with all of your heart. When you seek me with all of your heart, you will find the answers you seek and every good gift from a Father who loves you. When you seek me, the questions in your heart become the mountains that move upon my command.

I AM the answer.

I AM the truth. I AM your good Father.

 Lord, I receive the truth that you are my good Father and have good for me and all that I carry in my heart. I will share my questions right now, Father. Please grant unto me revelation to know how you are moving in these areas. Release your peace upon all my concerns and move with power to bring about your perfect will in each one. In Jesus' mighty name I pray. AMEN

28

REDEEMING PRINCE OF PEACE

> *And the peace of God, which passes all understanding, shall keep your hearts and minds through Christ Jesus.*

PHILIPPIANS 4:7

A word, harshly spoken.
The altering of what once was.

The pain of loss collides with the demand of unwanted change. Regret knocks upon the heart. Remorse follows close on the heels as the hope of restoration dims with the silence of unanswered pleas to be heard, be forgiven.

Beloved, I am here. I am your comfort in the pain. Bring the rejection before me. Place upon the altar injustice and robbery of your peace. I gently collect your tears, each a glimmer of a rendheart. I am present to walk with you as you face your fears.

My beloved, you were never intended to defeat this dragon named Offense and its blackguard partner, Bitterness. I stand in the gap of your gaping wound to shelter your innocence and bear the blows of grief and your pain.

I am Jesus.

My intentions toward you are eternal kindness, goodness, and love. I am your eternal friend. Forever, trustworthy, and true, loyal to stand at your side. Your pain, I defeat. I am your hope. I am restoration and redemption. I am the light directing your brave steps forward and I am the love that soothes your broken spirit.

My grace heals your wounding, and by my command, regret and remorse are banished to the abyss. I am an ever-present help. A door that opens to welcome you to new paths leading to wonder, wholeness, healing, and fulfillment.

Release your wounded emotions into my restorative hands. I bind up the brokenhearted and you will live, joyful. Lasting peace is my decree. My peace surpasses all understanding and peace shall fill your days and rule the nights.

 Oh Jesus, I believe in you. I receive all that you accomplished for me at the cross. I choose this day to step into the healing and wholehearted living you have for me today. I am choosing to see joy and peace surround me. As you provide your peace, I will share and release peace into the atmospheres where I live. Thank you, Jesus, for your faithfulness, for your goodness, and love. AMEN

29

ALL IS WELL, MY CHILD

> *Your eyes saw my unformed body; all the days ordained for me were written in your book before one of them came to be.*
>
> *PSALM 139:16*

Plan "B" does NOT exist in my realm.

Second best is as though—last.

Settling for a "less-than" life is a corrupted mindset.

I AM the God of intelligence, wonder, and perfection. You are my child, born into an inheritance of promise, beauty, and provision.

I knew you as you were being formed in your mother's womb, every human being, the entire human race. Each a perfect reflection of my love. You were not a mistake. You were not forgotten, ignored, or "less-than." Distortion entered in and swept away my designs, etched upon the pages of your book before time began. Plans to prosper you and give you a hope and a future.

My child, throw away this paltry plan B. In this hour choose to resurrect your aspirations, kept dormant. Take one step of bold courage, out of the mundane safety of obscurity. Choose today to live in your proper life. Desire to live out of the outlandish adventures, gifts of love, creative expression that are concealed under pain and fear.

Choose to live, fully alive!

Today, I liberate you from plan B. At this hour I recalibrate your original destination: truth, goodness, righteousness, peace, and joy (Romans 14:17). Redemption is at my core. Restoration, rediscovery, and rescue, all procured by my Son.

Choose my plan!

My script.

My direction.

My truth.

My VOICE!

Live wildly, unbridled, expectant, and fulfill the promises I kindly wrote about you millions of years ago.

Call out to me and I will amend, restore, and release.

All is well, my child. All is well.

 Father, I surrender my insecurities and plans that were constructed by my imagination that are outside of your perfect will for my life. Today, I ask you to restore to my life and the promises you wrote in my book before time began. I choose to dream with you. I expectantly wait to see your promises come forth. May all I do bring you glory. In Jesus' name. AMEN

30

PILLAR OF RIGHTEOUSNESS

> *The words "it was credited to him" were written not for him alone, but also for us, to whom God will credit righteousness—for us who believe in him who raised Jesus our Lord from the dead. He was delivered over to death for our sins and was raised to life for our justification.*

ROMANS 4:23-25

I credit you with righteousness!

I credit you with faithfulness.

You have persevered under circumstances and oppression that would break others. Yet, you have remained steadfast. The ground has shaken beneath your feet on multiple occasions. However, firm are your feet, as you have clung to the Cross.

Lies, accusation, swells of fear collided about you. But your faith in me remains untarnished, unbroken, and unwavering.

Then the fire! The blows of doubt, whispers of shame, confusion, failure licked as wicked tongues about your faith. I HEARD YOUR PRAYERS. I saw your tears and the breaking of your heart.

NO MORE!

My decree is spoken. My WORD given. The enemy is in retreat. The devil defeated.

You are credited with the gold of righteousness. You are welcomed in my Courts. You are a Pillar in my Kingdom. My sons and daughters, you now command the armies of the Living God.

Arise into the joy, purposes, and the position of your inheritance.

I credit you, Victorious!

 Abba, my heart fills with joy to understand how you view me. I give you thanks that you have walked with me through the flames of testing and have approved. Now I stand in the victory as a child of God and will make decrees for the angelic out of the great wisdom gained through the battle years. Thank you, Father, for your goodness and my inheritance. AMEN

31

UNCHAINED

> *Let us not become weary in doing good, for at the proper time we will reap a harvest if we do not give up.*

GALATIANS 6:9

For those who are in labor, contending in the battle for promises, new strategies, and relief, I sense Yahweh's urging.

Do not grow weary!

You stand upon the precipice of discovery. Significant and lasting changes and freedoms. The preparations have been met. Your obedience realized.

The angelic are readied, prepared. Movement over the next several days is imminent.

The words of prayer are nearing overflow. The scales of heaven are laden. The tipping point is NOW. The response, decreed.

Provision, answers, promises met are pouring out. Scrolls written and dispatched, within angelic hands.

The battle for the end rages.

Delivery is at hand and will not be thwarted.

Press in. Your faith is the key. Call forth that which is not as though it is.

> *God, who gives life to the dead and calls*
> *those things which do not exist as*
> *though they did.*
> —Romans 4:17 (NKJV)

Your perseverance is the substance of powerful prayer.

> *Let perseverance finish its work so that*
> *you may be mature and complete, not*
> *lacking anything.*
> —James 1:4 (NIV)

The season has arrived, and God is shifting the assignments, gifts, and future.

He is our good Father. BELIEVE and receive. For you shall see the goodness of the LORD in the land of the living.

The WORD of God cannot be chained!

 Lord, I thank you for how you continually remind me that my daily struggle will not destroy me. I lean into your truths that I will overcome if I don't become weary. Father, on the days that weariness seeks to take me down, be my rescue and

restoration. Fill me with heavenly energy and more than enough to accomplish all that is before me. Lord, I choose this moment to receive your goodness. Thank you, Father. AMEN

32

ONE MOMENT OF BRAVE FAITH

 I will guide you along the best pathway for your life. I will advise you and watch over you.

PSALM 32:8

My beloved child, would you this day take one step of bold faith? I entreat you; dare take my hand. Grasp the possibility of the promise which dawns upon the morrow. Release that which appears as an unchanging reality of your circumstances. Take one bold step into a spacious and unexpected moment of brilliant and brave faith, heralding your heart in belief for the miraculous.

Break free from the brutal taskmaster of your experience. Leaving far behind the comparisons silently construed from other's achievements and the expectations placed upon you by coworkers, siblings, neighbors, the echo of relationships long past. Today, reject the doomsayers provoking voices of fear, failure, and defeat, which leave you bereft and imprisoned in mundane living.

This is your beautiful, pristine moment of foretaste of the realm of possibility with me and uncover greater freedoms.

No judgement.

Unrestrained belief.

A hopeful future.

I am in all of these. I AM the freedom that your deserted soul is longing. Lay down your busyness for tranquil. Silence the comparisons and rest in my Word. For my words restore, refuel, recalibrate, redeem all that was stolen or lost. Rest in me this day. Dream and walk out the imagery of creativity, hope, and joy.

Take courage to release your authentic self to the world. You are not a mistake, nor have I abandoned you. You are a flawless expression of my love and beauty to many in and around your life. I bless you today. Reach for my hand and live out your destiny with joy, hope, and peace.

 Father, I receive your affirmation and your release to live out of my inner, authentic self. I believe you have rest, hope, joy, and peace assigned to my life. I will walk in this assurance. Lead me in the pathways for your name's sake. AMEN

33

MY SON HEALS ALL

> *He himself bore our sins in his body on the cross, so that we might die to sins and live for righteousness; "by his wounds you have been healed."*
>
> *1 PETER 2:24*

My child, fear not! The enemy has petitioned to sort through you—even unto death.

However, his petitions have been denied in the heavenly courts this very hour. Although he has hit you hard, the accuser WILL —NOT—PREVAIL!

For I have received the fruit of thy hands and count it as righteousness. Thusly, I have relayed unto you through the hands of the angelic forces, the healing balm of Gilead. This oil is sent forth for your protection and healing.

Behold! I am delivering your healing now. Do not doubt. Do not listen to those who walk with fear. Their voices pour forth from the spirits of doom—gloom—and pessimism.

Take charge! Today, decree the promises of my hand. Set them as edicts over yourself. Stand upon them. Speak them. Pray them back to me. Arise daily bearing witness that your healing progresses into finality.

Worship in the House of the LORD! Tell of my wonders. Reveal my promises. Stand in faith with the communion of the saints. The blood that is sprinkled speaks a better word than that of Abel. The blood covenant is mercy, grace, forgiveness, healing, and your wholeness.

All is well, my child.

I call you my beloved. You walk in my favor, hope, truth, and power. Decree my purposes forward in your life. You shall see my faithfulness unto all your petitions. And many will glory because you chose to believe.

Blessed are you among many, beloved child. I carry you in the very palm of my hand—the Lord, the LORD, God Almighty!

You did not choose me, but I chose you and appointed you so that you might go and bear fruit —fruit that will last—and so that whatever you ask in my name the Father will give you (John 15:16).

Praise the Lord, my soul; all my inmost being, praise his holy name. Praise the Lord, my soul, and forget not all his benefits— who forgives all your sins and heals all your diseases, who redeems your life from the pit and crowns you with love and compassion, who satisfies your desires with good things so that your youth is renewed like the eagle's (Psalm 103:1-5).

But he was pierced for our transgressions, he was crushed for our iniquities; the punishment that brought us peace was on him, and by his wounds we are healed (Isaiah 53:5).

Jesus saith unto him, "Rise, take up thy bed, and walk." And immediately the man was made whole, and took up his bed, and walked (John 5:8-9a).

A large crowd followed him, and he healed all who were ill (Matthew 12:15b).

> *Today, in the name of Jesus, I set a decree over myself for the complete healing of my body. I ask for healing specifically _____. Lord Jesus, by your name, blood, and authority, I stand upon the promises of God's Word and in faith to see all my petitions come forth. Thank you, Jesus. I worship you, the Father, and the Holy Spirit. AMEN*

A BLESSING FOR MOTHERS

> *Train up a child in the way he should go, and when he is old he will not depart from it.*

PROVERBS 22:6

I hear the cries of the mothers. Those who are raising babies and those who are pleading for their teens and those lamenting for the prodigals and all the children in between.

I hear the mama's cries in prayer, the spiritual mothers, those who are mentoring the next generation. I comprehend their hearts as they plead for those who are dear to their soul.

Know this now: I hear every word of intercession. The pleadings have reached my throne. I comprehend and am moved by their emotional petitions for protection. They stand as an impenetrable wall that shields their young from the onslaught of the demonic. They trample down the lies of deception that shout to them "defeat, doom, and destruction."

The prayers of love rise in a powerful wave that demands a release from heaven.

The angelic respond as I hear the petitions. I rise upon my Throne. My mothers of the faithful, I receive your petitions. Your children are my children.

I AM THEIR FATHER!

It is decreed: They will live and will not die.

They are the head and not the tail.

They will rise in victory and step fully into their divine calling which was prepared for them before the creation of the world.

And now my faithful mother of the Kingdom, I give you the rescue you are asking.

I bless you with refreshment.

I bless you with assurances.

I bless you with rest from your weariness of the battle.

I bless you with oil to dress your wounds and heal the young.

I bless you with a familial line, a heritage that is my inheritance for you and your children. Courage, holiness, sound mind, power, and wisdom. I bless you with grace, mercy, justice, peace, and joy in the Holy Spirit.

I bless you, mothers of the Kingdom of God!

Well done, good and faithful servants. Step into the joy of my Presence.

 Yahweh, I join you to pray for every mother who is petitioning for the salvation of a child. I stand with her and receive all these blessings for myself and all mothers. LORD, the cries of a mother's heart is reaching your Throne. Let us continue to bring before you those who are close to our soul. Move in

their lives to bless, protect, and bring them with fire and power into the Kingdom of Light. In Jesus' name. AMEN

35

MOUNTAIN OF FEAR MUST BOW

> *Do not be anxious about anything, but in every situation, by prayer and petition, with thanksgiving, present your requests to God. And the peace of God, which transcends all understanding, will guard your hearts and your minds in Christ Jesus.*
>
> *PHILIPPIANS 4:6-7*

My beloved child, when did you turn your eyes from mine? At what point did this mountain of adversity grow, overbearing, that its looming presence encroached upon your peace and well-being?

These emissaries of satan, cloaked in a cape of red pain and black fear, have drawn truth from your spirit. The threats of abandonment, poverty, and loss are screaming forward toward you from the summit of this mountain. The reality appears certain, as does your defeat.

Ah, but my beloved of God, it IS NOT SO!

Turn your faith back to me. Disengage the mountain and focus fully upon my love.

For I AM your Freedom Fighter. I AM your liberty!

This seemingly insurmountable climb before you is brought low in my Presence. I bring before your remembrance, your positioning as my child upon the earth and your stature. You are equipped with power from on high and are seen by the spiritual realm as royalty and joint heir with Christ. You carry ALL of my provision and protection which was purchased through the new blood covenant.

I speak to your soul this hour, Fear not! For I know the plans that I have for you, to give you a hope and a future. Therefore, arise and reclaim your truth. Speak to this mountain, "Go throw yourself into the sea." Believe in me.

The foreboding intruder into your life MUST bow to the name you bear, child of Yahweh.

Your freedom is at hand.

Your deliverance is at hand.

Your peace is your birthright and your banner and shield are love.

Jesus answered, "Truly I tell you, if anyone says to this mountain, 'Go, throw yourself into the sea,' and does not doubt in their heart but believes that what they say will happen, it will be done for them. Therefore, I tell you, whatever you ask for in prayer, believe that you have received it, and it will be yours. And when you stand praying, if you hold anything against anyone, forgive them, so that your Father in heaven may forgive you your sins.'" (Mark 11:22-25)

Father, in the name of Jesus, I come into complete agreement with my Kingdom identity. Thank you for bringing me into your truth as you always have. I will watch as you defeat my enemy, silence my accuser, and bring my rescue from those who have dishonored me. I receive my freedom this day, my deliverance, and I declare that I am shielded within your love. AMEN

36

WHEN YOU FACE CROSSROADS

> *Keep asking that the God of our Lord Jesus Christ, the glorious Father, may give you the Spirit of wisdom and revelation, so that you may know him better.*

EPHESIANS 1:17

At the crossroads you stand. I perceive your thoughts as you face the choices placed before you in this season. Each direction you have carefully considered. The well-traveled path, the wide gate, the path of mystery.

Which will you choose?

In these moments of choice and great circumstance, it weighs upon your soul, the loneliness. You look upon the future with great concerns, trepidation. You've been abandoned of wise counsel, any fellow sojourner that will shore up your selection of the best path to travel.

My child, bring each choice, each of these life decisions, before me. Place them in humble prayer before the Throne of Grace.

Pray the prayer of Apostle Paul. Keep asking that the God of our Lord Jesus Christ, the glorious Father, may give you the Spirit of Wisdom and Revelation, so that you may know me better.

Cease your striving and turn a listening ear; in the days, even hours, following your petitions, I will offer you the wisdom of heaven. You will proceed and live in my blessings.

Child, would you consider the possibility that it was I who created each choice for you? And perhaps each path holds unique blessings that will bring you joy, peace, and life? Choose now to refuse the whispers of distortion from the enemy of humanity. He will lie to entice you away on a detour of confusion and delay.

Pray with an earnest heart and ask for my wisdom. Then wait expectantly. I will direct your paths and they will lead to righteousness, peace, and joy in the Holy Spirit.

 Father, forgive me when I step out of peace and into strife and striving. I choose this hour to center myself in your truths and to seek your wisdom. I will face many decisions today that will have paths that can lead to life or to harm. I ask for your voice to guide me to choose the path that leads me into your presence and into wholehearted life. Thank you, Father, that I can always bring my choices and concerns before you without condemnation. I am free in your love. Thank you, Lord. AMEN

EXPECTATION IN PRAYER

> *In the morning, Lord, you hear my voice; in the morning I lay my requests before you and wait expectantly.*

PSALM 5:3

M y child, pray expectantly!

Learn from my son, David, who as a child, alone in the pastures of Israel, spoke to me at the dawning of the day. He carried this practice with him all the days of his life. David would cry out, "Listen to my voice in the morning, Lord." He would anticipate my responses with expectancy. And I would answer.

Child, step into wisdom. Pray upon the daybreak, presenting your heart, troubles, desires, and dreams before me and then believe excitedly. Walk into your day remembering the words you shared with me in the early morning.

Ruminate upon them as you work and play.

Then Behold!

As I move and commence to answer, supply, rearrange, complete your petitions—whisper your thanksgiving.

Be expectant of my replies, my instructions. Be expectant of love. Be expectant because I AM your good Father.

Ask and it will be given to you; seek and you will find; knock and the door will be opened to you (Matthew 7:7).

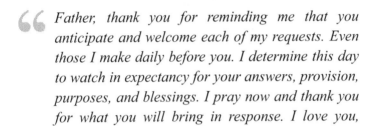

Father, thank you for reminding me that you anticipate and welcome each of my requests. Even those I make daily before you. I determine this day to watch in expectancy for your answers, provision, purposes, and blessings. I pray now and thank you for what you will bring in response. I love you, Father. You are good. AMEN

38

MANTLE OF BOLDNESS

> *You are the light of the world. A town built on a hill cannot be hidden. Neither do people light a lamp and put it under a bowl. Instead they put it on its stand, and it gives light to everyone in the house. In the same way, let your light shine before others, that they may see your good deeds and glorify your Father in heaven.*

MATTHEW 5:14-16

O ut of this dark and wicked world I choose you. Be my light.

I choose you to rise out of the shadows shouldered with a cloak of boldness. You may feel ill-equipped to stand against the shaming from a public that is raging against me, but I have released into you a spirit of confident peace. Remember my instructions in the book of Ephesians— STAND—just stand for me. I will do the fighting!

I have angels surrounding you. They fight for you at my command. Your words of prayer are strategic battle plans that activate the angelic realm.

This very hour in which you live, you are called to participate in one of the greatest moments of my Kingdom, the Acts 2 Church. This is a critical hour in the history of humanity. And…..

I chose you to see it.

I chose you to live it.

I chose you to pray it forth.

I chose you to prophesy my love, forgiveness, and mercy.

Take my hand, my child.

Stand with me, my heir of salvation.

I bequeath a spirit of boldness upon you!

You are more powerful than you believe, and your life and prayers are bringing the Light into the world this very hour.

Well done, my child. WELL DONE!

 Father, I receive this mantle of boldness. I choose to step into the high calling you have declared over my life. I accept and am thankful for the grand purposes you designed for me before time began. I receive the Spirit of Boldness and will be a light in my culture. Thank you, Father. AMEN

39

DEDICATE YOUR VOICE

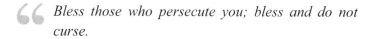

> *Bless those who persecute you; bless and do not curse.*

ROMANS 12:14

I AM not a God of unclean lips.

My words are faithful and true.

I do not speak forth shallow decrees. I speak and all of creation follows.

You are a people whose speech is of unclean lips. Where you have spoken harshly, rashly, unkind, or uncaring—repent. Reverse the course.

Be cleansed by the blood of my son, Jesus. His blood cleanses every tongue and every thought.

Speak life. Speak out your desires and hopes. Speak forth destinies over your future, your children, and nation. Bring forth the plans and purposes of my Kingdom.

I have blessed your lips for the deliverance of many. Bless and do not curse.

Today make your mission to bless yourself, your family, your neighbor, your church, and those in your communities with Kingdom joy, peace, and goodness.

 Father, in Jesus' name, I apply the blood to cleanse my lips. I take this opportunity to offer my lips and my speech to you. I dedicate my mouth to speak out your blessings. I will speak forth goodness, joy, and the Shalom of heaven. I choose to be a voice of truth and love. Thank you, Father, for speaking through me. In Jesus' name. AMEN

40

MAKE A MOMENT WITH ME

> *Come to me, all you who are weary and burdened, and I will give you rest.*

MATTHEW 11:28

I am not absent.

The holy scriptures tell you plainly, *Never will I leave you. Never will I forsake you* (Hebrews 13:5).

I AM all around you. I hold your hand throughout the day and often you are unaware. I walk next to you and in a crowd. I speak your name and angels move at my command for your favor and protection. But so many of my children don't feel or know my presence. They don't perceive that they are forcing me away.

Moment-by-moment every thought, each choice made, draws me closer, or conversely, thrusts me out. The thought-life beckons or banishes. But my heart longs to spend every hour with you.

Take a lesson from your puppy. You have watched her carefully, slowly, crawl upon your lap, even as you balance your Bible, journal, coffee, and more. She is unaware you have other priorities. She is only content to rest upon your hip and nudges your hand for affirmation.

Nudge my hand.

Crawl upon my lap.

Make a moment with me.

Come to me as a child. Allow my smile upon your face as we sit together in the Throne Room. Let me fill you with assurances, confidence, affirmations. And while you are beside me, there I will reveal treasures old and new. Glimpses of the blessings in your life upon the earth. I will whisper wisdom into your ear, and you will walk with certainty and love out of distraction, temptation, danger and into my perfect will.

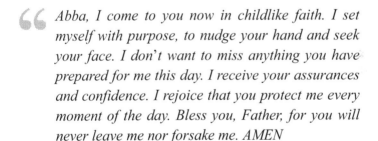

Abba, I come to you now in childlike faith. I set myself with purpose, to nudge your hand and seek your face. I don't want to miss anything you have prepared for me this day. I receive your assurances and confidence. I rejoice that you protect me every moment of the day. Bless you, Father, for you will never leave me nor forsake me. AMEN

41

LION'S ROAR

> Then one of the elders said to me, "Do not weep! See, the Lion of the tribe of Judah, the Root of David, has triumphed. He is able to open the scroll and its seven seals."

REVELATION 5:5

The ROAR of the Lion of Judah rends the heavens. The signal released, angelic armies advance.

The rescue of the faithful is at hand. The children of The Ancient of Days gather in multitudes, gazing toward the heavens in anticipation.

Behold, upon the clouds, shimmering golden, flashes of blue and white, illuminating the sky, the Lion appears. Regal, powerful, eyes of fire, filled with purpose. Worthy, the crown upon his brow. King of Kings displays as a medallion about his neck.

The lawless scream in terror as the sky splits in two. Confusion skitters the demonic into the crevices of the earth. The great and terrible day of the Lord is at hand as they stumble to flee the coming recompense.

The faithful stand, fearless. The Lion approaches, his authority flawless. And the faithful await knowing their liberation is assured, adorned in their mantle—Chosen of God!

The Great Day of the King dawns with the weighty judgement or with forgiveness, but its finality is undeniable.

The Lion, strong and mighty, thunders once more. The sifting commences. The countless step forth to receive their crowns; righteousness, sacrifice, obedience, faithfulness...

Everlasting peace and rest—the decree resonates forth. The Kingdom of God reigns forevermore.

Hallelujah. AMEN

 Jesus, I will behold you as you roar across the heavens. I thank you for the covenant you sealed with your blood. I eagerly await this triumphant day and I will stand without fear. I will be those whom you count faithful. I will worship and bow down and set my crown at your feet. Thank you, Jesus. I praise you this day. AMEN

42

I AM THE GREAT I AM

> *Let the redeemed of the Lord say so, whom he hath redeemed from the hand of the enemy.*

PSALM 107:2

I AM your hope.

I AM every moment of peace.

I AM your strength, your happy place.

I am not absent as you suppose. Dwell not on the climate of lawlessness, the churning deception of hatred and bitterness. These are merely ploys put forth by the ruler of the air designed with intent to snare and imprison. I laugh at such childish ramblings of the arrogant. It is written: As surely as I live, every knee will bow before me, every tongue will acknowledge God.

Rest in peaceful assurance that promises given are promises kept.

I watch from my throne and I listen to each sincere prayer. I'm moved by your humility and the words lifted before me. I listen intently to utterances for your family, health, your community, and nation.

Pray! Because your words bring light and truth to humanity. Pray, and wait upon the Spirit.

I am not distant and unconcerned. You shall be a witness to the greatest move of God that is prepared for this season.

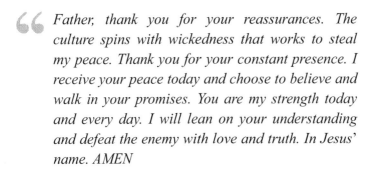

Father, thank you for your reassurances. The culture spins with wickedness that works to steal my peace. Thank you for your constant presence. I receive your peace today and choose to believe and walk in your promises. You are my strength today and every day. I will lean on your understanding and defeat the enemy with love and truth. In Jesus' name. AMEN

43

LET MY WORDS DEFINE YOU

 Sanctify them by the truth; your word is truth.
JOHN 17:17

L et my words define your value.

Lean not into the changing winds of social constructs, push back the words and lies that a broken parent left upon you. Exchange harsh untruths that were flung and stung from across the room by a spouse or a friend and receive peace. Reject the words of unworthiness, unloved, unqualified, and unfavorable.

Let my WORD define you!

I have much to say about you. I adore you. I am with you and will never abandon you. You are my beloved, my child, and a fountain of life. My Word is truth and my Word is life.

Breathe me in and live.

Wholly, holy, fully, and without fear. Let my Words surround you, edify you, and fulfill your destiny in this hour. You are chosen, beloved, free, powerful, strong, and wise! Live forth from these Words and the world around you will thus live by your definition and thus mine.

Hallelujah!!

 Your Words are truth. I choose today to surrender word curses spoken over me by people who had the capacity to hurt and harm me. I forgive them. I give them over to you along with words that wounded my soul. I receive the healing love and truth as a covering to heal my pain. And out of my healing, I offer forgiveness and choose to bless those that stung with words in my past. Thank you, Lord, that you define me. That is where I choose to dwell. Thank you for the peace and joy that come from your Words over my life. In Jesus' name. AMEN

44

TESTIMONY

> *Publish his glorious deeds among the nations. Tell everyone about the amazing things he does.*
>
> *PSALM 96:3*

Kingdom Writers: I sense the urgency of the LORD this morning.

The word *testimony* is ringing in the heavenlies. It's our season to write our story, to publish his deeds among the nations. Now is the right time to release the book that the LORD has placed within, onto the screen. It is the fullness of time, to bring it forth, and for your powerful voice to be shared among the peoples of God. The time is at hand, declares the LORD, to impart my faithfulness, healing, and freedom. Reveal to the world what Jesus' blood has purchased at the highest price.

Do not delay.

Angelic assignments are coming forth from heaven with writing prompts to organize your thoughts and words and thusly release your story to the nations. Blessings are assigned upon your writings. No more delay; over your time, energy, and creativity. Write for the Kingdom and bring honor to his name.

 Father, I have a story that you birthed within. Help me to view my story as a testimony that will bring your love and healing to others. I receive the blessings and the angelic assistance to release my story. Father, I ask your hand of favor over it. Lead me to the right place and people where I can share my story and bring you honor. In Jesus' name I pray. AMEN

45

CALLING ALL MISFITS

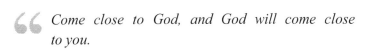 *Come close to God, and God will come close to you.*

JAMES 4:8a

I AM calling the misfits of the Kingdom. Those of my children who have longed to be at the center of life. Those who have given their hearts to me through long seasons of brokenhearted prayer.

I have heard your pleadings. The tears of anguish as you were judged, then punished for the crimes against you. Crimes you didn't commit but endured as bludgeoning of the devil and at the hands of others. The trauma marked you in the eyes of humanity —unworthy, questionable, unreasonable.

But hear me now!

All that have watched through the glass window, peering into the life which you long to participate, longing for a scrap of acceptance, pleading for your voice to be heard....

I CHOOSE YOU!

Out of the embers of your forgotten pain, YOU.... WILL.... RISE!

I choose you.

From the years of faithful prayer, emerging in power, and Holy Spirit covering, you will take back territory lost years ago that the others failed to recapture. The stunned look on the bystanders will be displayed on faces of those incredulous of my choosing.

I choose you.

The many who have served me faithfully yet, left unrewarded. The men and women banished from the ordinary. My children who look with different eyes upon the broken, bleeding souls with genuine love and acceptance and supernatural compassion.

I choose you.

Take up your mantle. See my Kingdom forward. Forgive those who forced you out. You gained much from your misfit years. You now possess many secrets of the Kingdom. This is the new Kingdom proclamation of the angelic shouting. Behold, the rising of my misfits. And my child, you fit perfectly.

Well done, my child, well done. Prepare now, for the Kingdom of God is near.

 Thank you, Father, that you have watched and walked with me throughout the years I felt left out and forgotten. Thank you for perceiving my pain and confusion. Thank you for never leaving me and granting me wisdom in those years of pain. Thank you I am chosen. I choose you, Father. I will always serve your Kingdom and I will rise and

reflect your glory. In my Savior's name, Jesus, AMEN

46

THE NEW KINGDOM AGE

> For I am about to do something new. See, I have already begun! Do you not see it? I will make a pathway through the wilderness. I will create rivers in the dry wasteland.
>
> *ISAIAH 43:19*

The sound of a mighty trumpet blast!

The roar of the Lion of Judah reverberates through the halls of antiquity. All of heaven rises in honor, as the Lion of Judah, the King of Kings, strides to the timeline of humanity. The timepiece, ever-present, before the Throne of Grace.

A christening of the new era, KINGDOM!

Decrees of completion, as the age of the church of man, reaches conclusion. Humanity's philosophies, incomplete but blessed with love, enduring for centuries, the testimonies of redemption. Yet, religion without true holiness remained inadequate to represent and reveal the resplendent God of the universe.

The Trumpet of the Ram's horn expresses; Kingdom revelation is at hand. The Kingdom of God, on earth as it is in heaven. Flashes of fire, as people step boldly into the new season, adorned with brilliant realities, few anticipated until now.

Healing, the stripes on his back, fully alive and available.

Trust, I AM that I AM, the voice of wholeness which is the answer to every difficulty facing humanity.

Peace, as the supernatural river of life flows through the people of God.

The Holy One, Ancient of Days, now releasing signs, wonders, and the miraculous into the earth through his people. The great army prepared, those groomed in the church age joined with the newly saved and the angelic, all shout: Hallelujah! The day of the Lord! The Kingdom of Yeshua is at hand!

The table of feasts is adorned, prepared for those who desire more. The Kingdom of the Most High is advancing in innovation, the likes unseen prior to this day.

Behold!

Be astonished. Blessings abound in the new season, for great is his loving-kindness to this generation. HALLELUJAH!

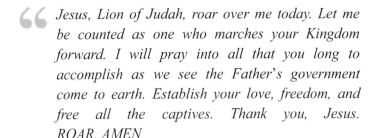

> *Jesus, Lion of Judah, roar over me today. Let me be counted as one who marches your Kingdom forward. I will pray into all that you long to accomplish as we see the Father's government come to earth. Establish your love, freedom, and free all the captives. Thank you, Jesus. ROAR. AMEN*

47

JEHOVAH-RAPHA TRUTH

" *For how much more will I, your Father, who is in heaven give good things to my children, who ask of me?*

MATTHEW 7:11b

My beloved child, you are anxious to rush into the day.

But wait. Linger, tarry a moment longer in my presence. Wholly focus on my voice in this hour.

Allow the love of your good Father to fall upon your heart. Allow my love to counsel your mind and the wisdom of your discerning for all that you face at the moment.

Wait in the quiet and behold my name, Jehovah-Rapha: I AM the God who heals.

Lay down the doom and gloom that trounces upon your mind and perceived future. That is not of my realm. Cast off the curses of death and disease. Release the lie that eats upon your soul that your illness belongs to you or that your circumstance is hopeless.

Reject the deception that you must continually contend with relentless wickedness. This device is of my enemy and not of my hand.

Linger here in the secret place. Petition your healing. Seek my holiness. Knock upon the door of truth. Declare my name, Jehovah-Rapha over the pain, disillusionment, over unbelief and doubt. Declare truths of who I AM:

I AM good!

I AM faithful.

I AM powerful

I AM Jehovah-Rapha

Your healer.

Now, walk into your life, expectant.

Behold all that opens unto you.

 Father, I will declare your truths over me, my body, my circumstance. You are always my good Father. You are faithful and will never leave me. You are powerful and able to accomplish all things. You, Father, are Jehovah-Rapha, my healer. I today petition for my complete healing. I declare over myself and bless myself with divine health. In Jesus' name. AMEN

48

STAND DOWN SPIRIT OF FEAR

> *So shall they fear the name of the Lord from the west, and His glory from the rising of the sun; when the enemy comes in like a flood, the Spirit of the Lord will lift up a standard against him.*

ISAIAH 59:19

Today I decree an edict from heaven's halls. Stand down spirit of fear! Stand down spirit of lawlessness. Stand down spirit of infirmity, sickness, cancer, disease. Stand down confusion, depression, anxiety, and immorality.

For my God will come in like a flood. He will raise up a Standard against you and the armies of the Living God will bind you and cast you into the pit. In the name of King Jesus. AMEN!

Hallelujah AMEN. God is shouting this verse over the entire earth and his church. AMEN

> *Speak your purposes from heaven. Father, let your church, the church of the firstborn of Christ Jesus,*

echo back your desires. I join my prayers with the angels to defeat the demonic realm and to release peace, healing, and courage across the earth. Father, I will decree your words into my own life and watch as you defeat my enemies. I join with Jesus who will march them before you in a victory parade. AMEN

49

I AM IN YOUR CORNER AND ON YOUR SIDE

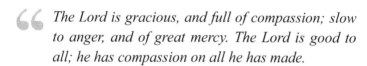

> *The Lord is gracious, and full of compassion; slow to anger, and of great mercy. The Lord is good to all; he has compassion on all he has made.*

PSALM 145:8-9

The world rages.

I AM tenderness.

Harsh words sting your soul.

I AM kindness.

Filth spews through the airwaves.

I AM pure.

Fear swirls in greater depths. Distrust, vengefulness, and lawlessness sweep the land.

But…. I remain Sovereign. I AM.

I AM in your corner.

I AM by your side.

Choose me this hour and receive my tenderness. Let my compassion scrape away the crusty scabs that lengthen over your hopes and dreams—over your heart.

I AM:

Your protector.

Your advocate.

Your defender.

Your provider.

Your lover.

Your peace giver.

I AM always with you. Even in the pain of hurtful words, of a world embroiled with rage. I AM your healer, hope, and strong tower.

Run to me this hour. I AM in your corner and on your side.

Bring your wounds, your lost opportunities, and lost hopes to me. My tenderness will heal, release, and realize all the plans I decree over your life.

I AM your God. My plans are to prosper you and not to harm you, plans to give you a hope and a future.

I AM in your corner today and I AM on your side. Try me in this and watch what I will do.

 Father, I am humbled today to comprehend that you are all things to me. These words of love ring

powerful in my heart today as I face uncertainty. I know you have goodness for my life. I believe! I receive your truths and promises. I know you are on my side. Thank you, Father. You are so good to me. Thank you. AMEN

I AM THE COLLECTOR

> *Love is patient, love is kind. It does not envy, it does not boast, it is not proud. It does not dishonor others, it is not self-seeking, it is not easily angered, it keeps no record of wrongs. Love does not delight in evil but rejoices with the truth. It always protects, always trusts, always hopes, always perseveres.*
>
> *1 CORINTHIANS 13:4-7*

Lost friendships, broken marriages, sons and daughters-defiant, those who are aloof, and those estranged from fathers and mothers. Hearts of humanity poured out love upon others and gave their essence of trust and priority. All in, they placed tenderness, faith, and vulnerability into the hands of another.

The lure of another, the misty promise of greener pastures in distant places, they are the lies that twist and deceive. The voice of whispered temptation alluring as a clarion call, there is something out there, another soul who will fill the loneliness, soothe the self-loathing, the turmoil that roils within.

Temptation knocks on the door and enters in.

Carnage of broken lives left abandoned by the wayside.

But I am the collector. I am the salvager of brokenness and healer of hearts. Open the door to my love. I rush in like a flood, soothing the torn and bleeding soul. My hope gently cascades and fills every empty space. Peace and assurance are the balm of healing.

I AM your strong tower and I will defend you. My sword is poised, and angels aligned into place. I AM the blessing of peace, joy, and goodness. I will heal, redeem, and I am your greatest adventure.

Place my love and truths as your foundation and anything is possible. Freedom, courage, strength, wisdom, and yes, even reconciliation is probable.

I am your future and it is my relentless intention to fill every open place left empty by another. Knock and see. Taste and know that I AM a good Father.

 Father, you are the collector and I believe you are able and willing to salvage all the brokenness of my heart and the hearts of those whom I love. I choose this day to open my heart-gate to you. Come rushing in like a flood and heal. Place within me your laughter. Show me how to bring your healing to this lost and broken world. I ask all this in the name of Jesus. AMEN

51

THE ATMOSPHERE OF HEAVEN ON EARTH

> *You will keep in perfect peace those whose minds*
> *are steadfast, because they trust in you.*

ISAIAH 26:3

Shalom… Shalom… Shalom

I shout over the earth, Shalom!

I AM Shalom.

I AM the Shalom, peace.

I AM the Shalom, harmony.

I AM the Shalom, prosperity.

I AM the Shalom, welfare.

I AM the Shalom, tranquility.

I AM the hello in the morning and the Shalom of the evening.

It is out of perfect peace that your strength is born, your might is evidenced, and the wisdom and power of the Holy Spirit displayed. The perfect Shalom of God is an impenetrable wall that thwarts anxiety, defeats depression, and Shalom defeats chaos, deception, division, and powerlessness.

Shalom cancels assignments of the enemy and throws down every lofty pretense that comes against the knowledge and standard of God!

Speak Shalom over your life today. Test me in this.

I AM YOUR SHALOM!

 Father, you are the Shalom that is my protection. I ask for your peace to surround me today. I choose to live and dwell in peace and rest. Within this atmosphere I can do all things in Christ Jesus. I receive the Shalom of heaven today in my mind, will, and emotions. I receive your peace in my body, soul, and spirit. In the powerful name of Jesus. AMEN

52

I BECKON, COME!

> Because of the Lord's great love we are not
> consumed, for his compassions never fail. They are
> new every morning; great is your faithfulness.

LAMENTATIONS 3:22-23

I beckon you, COME!

Come walk with me in the early morning among the vineyards, the fields, the parks, or along the water. Come and BEHOLD!

Behold my face in the beauty of my natural creation. Take in the wonder and splendor of the twinkling dews upon the twining branches. Catch glimpses of my glory prepared intimately for you.

Perfumed breezes. Breathe in and fill your soul with the promise of renewal. I am washing away the old, the tired, the grim, the broken and will carry your burden. Behold the newness of the dawn. Streams of light flit across the sky through bundled clouds laden with the promise of showers. Brilliance smiles down. She boasts of the awaiting hours pregnant with hope, possibilities, and wonder.

This is a morning of promise.

Dare to dream again. I am resolute to restore the aspirations of your heart; hope, memories, imaginings, and creativity which were crushed by the blows of a brutal world.

I AM your Father who established your dreams before time began. Each written into the scroll of your life. It is my will to redeem each one and then bless you to walk fully into the aspirations of your future.

Step into the natural world this morning and partake, my child. Make time for me. I will renew your hope.

I beckon you, walk with me this day and receive the depth, width, breadth of my love and goodness.

 Lord, I look at the beauty contained within the natural world and see your creativity and your peace. I will join you there and receive the blessing of standing in your presence. Let me always look upon the sky, the trees, and your creation with awe and wonder. Allow me to always perceive your goodness and love through the natural world. I ask that when I meet with you in nature that you will always delight. Thank you, Father. AMEN

53

ENRAPTURED

66 *God is our refuge and strength, an ever-present help in trouble.*

PSALM 46:1

I AM omnipresent. I live all around you. I am the voice of hope within. The peace that arrives in the morning. My love powers the universe and it is the gentle whisper of grace in the smile of a child, a warm embrace of a friend, and the truth that ushers in freedom to the downtrodden.

In your moments of doubt, arrest your thoughts with the truth. The knowledge of my ever-present reality. I AM with you always, even until the end of the age.

My Son purchased your life and eternity. His wisdom and promises are recorded in the Word. My promises are an ever-present blessing and guide throughout the generations. Believe and behold! You are only a breath, a word, a prayer away from the destiny I have prepared for you before time began.

My child, allow my presence to enrapture your heart. Discover the truth of my surrounding presence. Experience the attributes of life well lived, the economies of heaven, peace, fullness of joy, and righteousness.

Knock on the door of my Kingdom. Seek and you shall find. Look intently with persistence, you *will* discover the great, I AM.

I AM ubiquity.

I AM your ever-present hope.

 Father, I desire to experience the qualities of a life well lived. Today, I choose to position myself under your wings of protection. Father, align my heart, soul, body, and spirit to receive the provision of heaven. Teach me to consistently walk in peace, joy, and righteousness. I declare, you are my ever-present hope for all that I face today. I will live out of these truths and the victory that Jesus purchased at the cross. Thank you, Father. Thank you, Jesus. Thank you, Holy Spirit. AMEN

54

HOPE NATIONS SONG

> *He who has an ear, let him hear what the Spirit says to the churches. To him who overcomes, I will grant to eat of the tree of life which is in the Paradise of God.*

REVELATION 2:7

Come away with me.

Create the time and be free.

Leave the chaos of the day.

Step into my world, let's play.

I am for you. In my presence you thrive.

It is my pleasure to teach you that you needn't strive.

I place in your hand, keys to open my gifts, large and small.

Angelic are standing, awaiting your call.

Feathers floating, keys to behold.

Your story is written, now let it be told.

Angelic are standing, awaiting your call.

A child of God, steady, determined, you will not fall.

One slash of the sword, going forth from my mouth.

Angel armies arising, marching in from the south.

The enemy screeches, scrambling away in fear.

The Kingdom of God is certain and has now come near.

Raise the Banner higher, the Kingdom has come.

My people are healed, delivered with hope for the nations.

Forever aligned to Jesus, the Son.

The victory at hand, the battle is won!

> *Lord, I determine to step away from the chaos and striving. It's in your love that I am equipped to step into these great adventures and callings you have prepared for me. I trust you with my life. I dedicate my lips to speak forth your truths and purposes. I long to see the healing and hope for the nations. Use me to bring forth your Kingdom through the Lord Jesus Christ. AMEN*

55

AS IT IS IN HEAVEN

> *Your kingdom come, your will be done, on earth as it is in heaven.*

MATTHEW 6:10

The Armies of the Living God shout. Can you hear it?

The voice in the distance, from a whisper in the wilderness, is now arising.

The decree: On earth as it is in heaven.

Upon the tongue of every believer. Over and over and again. The saints shout in unity—through intercession, reaching a heroic force as their voice echoes, then repeats the cry of the angels, en masse:

On earth as it is in heaven!

The demons lurch under the onslaught of the consecrated sound. Their furious efforts of hate, division, and destruction fortify.

In reply, the saint's voices intensify, louder:

On Earth As It Is In Heaven!

The edict declared over and greater still. The sound fills the universe arriving at the pinnacle, a holy crescendo. The sound shouts down the demonic in a single day. This holy chant, loud and proud, full of faith and power.

ON EARTH AS IT IS IN HEAVEN!

The day of the decree is NOW. We wait in eager anticipation as God is poised, on the precipice.

It's Revival.

A Revolution.

Bring it forth, the faithful of Christ. Shout it out this hour:

On Earth As It Is In Heaven!

The clouds part, the sky rolls up, silence breaks.

Behold, THE LAMB OF GOD!

 In the name of Jesus Christ, I join in this holy decree. I declare the Kingdom of God here NOW, on earth as it is in heaven. I declare that every knee will bow to the name of Jesus Christ in the heavens, on the earth and under the earth. Let the revival begin, Lord Jesus. AMEN

HEALING BROKEN HEARTS

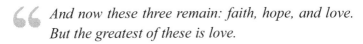 *And now these three remain: faith, hope, and love. But the greatest of these is love.*

1 CORINTHIANS 13:13

B ut Love:

Love is forever.

Love is our power to change darkness into light and struggle into victory!

Love can heal the heart, restore the body, and deliver the mind.

Love can cover a multitude of missteps, failed relationships, diminished hopes, and the ugliness of sin. Love heals our past, fills our present, and always facilitates our future.

Love reaches across boundaries of fear, across the street, the country, and love crosses generations.

Love will leave the ninety-nine to gather the one in its arms.

Love raises the dead and seats ordinary people as royalty in the heavenly realms with Christ.

Begin to whisper love. Then speak aloud. Bless strangers in the marketplace, at school, work, and church. Say I love you to your city, your neighbor and country.

Love your dog. Bless your cat! Step outside and shout to the Lord, "I love this beautiful world you gave me."

Bless it!

Transform it.

Within you rests the most powerful substance of healing and hope!

...And the greatest of these is...LOVE!

 Father, out of your great love let me speak love into this world. Wrap me in your love with fierce security. With your love it's always possible to love the un-lovely in my life. I can change my home, my community, and the lives of others through your love. Love always triumphs over fear. I choose love, today. I choose you. In Jesus' name. AMEN

ARISE, STRONG AND VICTORIOUS

> *But those who hope in the Lord will renew their strength. They will soar on wings like eagles; they will run and not grow weary, they will walk and not be faint.*
>
> *ISAIAH 40:31*

I am a holy child of The Most High!

I am seated among the heavens, clothed in glory, with Christ. Gossamer wings upon my spirit that ascend and set me to soar, like the eagles.

I have my Father's heart, his approval, his trust, power, and purposes at my right hand. I will trample the scorpions and snakes and every lie beneath my feet and then pull my brothers and sisters from the mouth of the dragon.

FREEDOM I shout! Freedom I speak to the nations. Honor and dignity to the people.

Set upon a hill, a light to all. This is the mandate of heaven. Rise sons and daughters, strong and tall. You have overcome the world by the word of your testimony through the redemption and blood of Jesus Christ.

Your inheritance is at hand! HALLELUJAH!

 Lord, my Father, in Jesus' name I thank you for adopting me and for a rich inheritance that I'm merely beginning to perceive and step into. Thank you for giving me your heart, trust, power and determining my life to accomplish your purposes. Lead me today to others who are struggling for their freedom. Reveal to me how to love them well and reveal their inheritance. AMEN

58

GOLDEN GLOBES

> *They lay their crowns before the throne and say:
> "You are worthy, our Lord and God, to receive
> glory and honor and power, for you created all
> things, and by your will they were created and have
> their being."*

REVELATION 4:10b-11

Kingdom Golden Globes, our spheres of honor, accolades given, bestowed by our Father. Ribbons, awards, positions bestowed in response to our sacrifice and the laying down of our hearts, prayers, service, and giving of gifts, and finances.

Blessings forevermore.

Redemption of hearts.

Restoration of relationships.

Strength to the feeble.

Vitality to the sick.

Everlasting life.

The Golden Globes of the Kingdom are the testimonies of the saints. The Crowns of Gold and glory, won on the battlefield of life. The very crowns which one day we'll throw at the feet of the King!

Saints walk the red carpet. It is the path "Less Taken." Stained by the blood of sanctification. Standing regal in gowns of glittering gold and brilliant white. Sashes of honor on display, crossing the chest, reflecting our love and loyalty to our Father. Jewels of perfection placed within the mantles that drape shoulders, reflecting a lifetime of giving, love, sacrifice for others on earth.

Golden Globes are bestowed as living ornaments that declare for all eternity,

OUR GOD IS GOOD!

His name be praised forever, Yahweh! Yeshua!

At the name of Yeshua every knee should bow, of those in heaven, and of those on earth, and of those under the earth. And that every tongue should confess that Jesus Christ is Lord to the glory of God the Father. AMEN

 Yeshua, you gave me honor and a crown of life. All the amazing ornaments of honor I dedicate to you and set my crowns at the feet of our Father. I bow my knee and give you thanks for how you have saved me, then honored me with gold. Thank you, Jesus, for how you sacrificed for me to walk in your honor and glory. AMEN

59

GOD'S VALIANT STAND —WATCH YOUR ENEMY'S DEFEAT

 Whoever dwells in the shelter of the Most High will rest in the shadow of the Almighty.

I will say of the Lord, "He is my refuge and my fortress, my God, in whom I trust."

Surely he will save you from the fowler's snare and from the deadly pestilence.

He will cover you with his feathers, and under his wings you will find refuge; his faithfulness will be your shield and rampart.

You will not fear the terror of night, nor the arrow that flies by day, nor the pestilence that stalks in the darkness, nor the plague that destroys at midday.

A thousand may fall at your side, ten thousand at your right hand, but it will not come near you.

You will only observe with your eyes and see the punishment of the wicked.

If you say, "The Lord is my refuge," and you make the Most High your dwelling, no harm will overtake you, no disaster will come near your tent.

For he will command his angels concerning you to guard you in all your ways; they will lift you up in their hands, so that you will not strike your foot against a stone.

You will tread on the lion and the cobra; you will trample the great lion and the serpent.

"Because he loves me," says the Lord, "I will rescue him; I will protect him, for he acknowledges my name.

He will call on me, and I will answer him; I will be with him in trouble, I will deliver him and honor him.

With long life I will satisfy him and show him my salvation."

PSALM 91

M y Child, you have valiantly faced the battles that continually arose before you. The clang of your sword echoes in the Halls of Heaven's Courts. The relentless assignment of demonic ministry has left you teary and weary.

But as you rise early watching as the light of morning dawns brave and hopeful, hear my decree for this season you have walked.

I SHALL AVENGE YOU!

Sheath the sword today and step under my covering. I go before you this day. Vengeance against your assassins is-now-MINE.

Listen to the angelic army arise, millions stand at attention, battle ready. They march forward with the display of my royal scepter. They are preceded into the battle theater by a blazing fire, the LION'S fierce roar of justice. The tsunamis of Living Water follow close at hand, scalding the principalities who desire to tether you to fear and powerlessness.

BEHOLD!

Today is your rescue!

I'm pushing back the darkness. The blood of the Lamb stamps all prisoners: FREE! Paid in full, crimson upon every demonic contract and curse. Your children are released, your marriage made whole, the dreams held buried deep in your childlike faith emerging into possibility.

I, the Lord God, will battle for you. I am for you. You merely need to stand, pray, and perceive the destruction of all that opposes. I grant unto you, my child, a warrior's blessing for standing your ground within the conflicts.

Creative thought, brilliant words, and authority are granted to rule over circumstances that once proved powerless. I bless your voice with strength and your mind with clarity.

YOU DID NOT GIVE UP!

You didn't waiver in choosing each and every time to honor your calling over comfort, love over pain, peace over fear.

Dignity and honor display upon the sash across your heart. Now, stand and view the destruction of thine enemies. Enter into the peace of your Father's Kingdom.

 Oh, Father God, I believe! I will stand and watch as you rescue me from the curses and devices of

our enemy. Lord, I receive with deep thanksgiving all that you are declaring over my life. Thank you, Father. I wait expectantly as you move, and I will share with many your faithfulness and love. AMEN

THE SIDE DOOR

> *These are the words of him who is holy and true,*
> *who holds the key of David. What he opens no one*
> *can shut, and what he shuts no one can open.*

REVELATION 3:7

In this moment, imagine you and Jesus are standing outside of a door. It's a large swinging door on hinges. A circular window is in the middle, much like a restaurant kitchen galley door.

Step up and peer through the window. There you catch a glimpse of a massive throne. Extravagant, gleaming, and towering. Looking up into the mist and the shimmer that surrounds the throne, seek the image of the Ancient of Days, he is seated upon this place, The Mercy Seat.

Then glance to the foot of the throne where brilliant and gleaming marble steps lead upward. And there discover people and angels in joyful assembly in eternal worship. It's bright and colorful and you are met with harmonies swirling in melodies of love from the room. The twinkle of the atmosphere is hope, made tangible.

Now, turn your attention back to the door in which you are peering and then look to your side at Jesus. Look into his eyes of love. He smiles and nods your welcome as he pushes the door open and takes you by the hand. Stepping forward with great anticipation and thrill, Jesus leads you to the foot of the Throne. Behold, you step into the presence. All is well. All is well.

 Oh Jesus, you are the door of entry. Thank you for welcoming me into this holy space. I will stand with you before the throne and give our Father glory and worship. I'm overwhelmed at the honor and privilege that you bestow. Thank you, Jesus.

61

FEAR IS DEFEATED

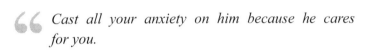

> *Cast all your anxiety on him because he cares for you.*
>
> *1 PETER 5:7*

My child, in the moments when fear rises and surrounds you on every side, don't look into its eyes of darkness. Refrain from entertaining the imaginations of *what if...* These scenarios of impending disasters and pain that tumble, one upon another, in your mind are weapons of my enemy. Darkened thoughts are engineered with intention and detail to trip you up.

They exhaust your hope, your faith, and your body, then deplete your soul of confidence and love.

When hopelessness looms, remember me, your Father in heaven. I always have a better path for your future. I am your good Father. I've prepared a way. A door will be opened unto you. A window of light will crack. Choose to look up. Look into my eyes of love. Behold, I possess every answer to every problem you face. Nothing is too difficult for me, my child, and my love will lead you, protect you, and bless you.

Pray against the gloom of fear. Shout the name of my son, Jesus, to your pain and worry. Your voice carries great power when you trust in me. I assure you that I will never leave you nor forsake you.

Deny the darkness all satisfaction. Command it to depart and welcome my love, truth, and light to walk you forward into the abundant life in Christ Jesus.

 Father, the enemy is relentless to whisper lies that steal my hope and faith. I praise you because you are always the voice of hope and my center. I listen to your voice and I reject the fear that is lingering with doubt. I will stand with you in truth and watch the door of breakthrough open before me. I will see your goodness in my life and watch as you provide the answers to all my questions and provision for my every need. Bless you, Father. Thank you. AMEN

62

WINDS OF CHANGE

> *And because we are his children, God has sent the Spirit of his Son into our hearts, prompting us to call out, "Abba, Father." Now you are no longer a slave but God's own child. And since you are his child, God has made you his heir.*

GALATIANS 4:6-7

M y beloved child, you are entering a new season, an unfolding of hope and new possibilities dispatched from my Throne and carried unto you by the angel, The Winds of Change. The assignment matches the greatness of your destiny that has been written in your book since before time began. It bears the weightiness of the glory yet to be revealed and will illuminate the gold of your past disappointments and pain.

The birth of your new commissioning is near, upon the door-posts, yet the pangs of transition are tremendous. The letting go of the old—the release of lost ideas, failed expectations, and the surrender of places and faces unrealized, bears down. I know your heart and have witnessed every tear and the years of unrealized reconciliation. It feels as though your earnest pleadings have died, fleeting as a vapor, unseeingly and unheard.

But I assure you, my beloved, I heard every word.

You are walking in a season of closure yet in tandem also with a moment of birthing. The confusion sent by the accuser of the brethren, arises with the mad intention of a tornado around you.

DO NOT LISTEN!

I stand as your Family Redeemer between the madness and confusion and peace and safety. You are not alone in this season of change. No, I will lift you up and out of the fear and place you firmly upon the path of holiness.

I will cover and soothe those lost hopes of yesterday. I will redeem every prayer and I hold and heal your broken heart. It's a season of change and release. Give to me your past. Your determination to continue to carry the past will inhibit your capacity to walk fully into the new places and greet new faces that await.

In this season of change, grip my hand, surrender the old. I will lead you through this birth, because the new dreams will be my greatest work yet in your life!

I bless you today to engage with the Winds of Change and receive every good gift from the Kingdom!

 Speak truth my child. Pray it aloud:

I am a child of The Most High.

I will listen to your voice.

You are always good, God!

You have only good things for me.

I will live bravely in your presence.

I receive your good gifts for this next season!

HALLELUJAH!

63

THE RESURRECTION —THE CENTRALITY OF LOVE

> *By this everyone will know that you are my disciples, if you love one another.*
>
> *JOHN 13:35*

Consider the love in the heart of Christ that he willingly offered himself to be brutally beaten for you and nailed on a tree. Let your soul be moved with emotion and purpose to love others, to forgive freely, to speak life and not death, to include, to be the hands, feet, and voice of our Father. Christ paid a very high price.

The profound implication of the Resurrection is far greater than most believers set aside time to reconcile. Powerful and life-changing gifts were bestowed upon this generation through the covenant that Jesus sealed upon the Cross. Child, you are honor-bound as benefactor of the spilled blood of Christ, knowing who you are and whose you are, destined to love well.

What does love look like?

Love is long-suffering.

Love is kind.

Love is humble.

Love is forgiveness.

Love is vulnerability.

Love always places connection with another as the highest goal.

Love is brave communication.

Love removes condemnation and releases honesty.

Love is the wellspring that flows from our heart.

Love is laying down the need to always be right.

Love is giving away your heart with the risk of betrayal.

Love heals, love restores, love triumphs, and love is our foundation.

Love is everything good from the Father's heart.

Love restores a single life and love redeems nations.

Let the Bride lock arms together. She has something that families, neighborhoods, nations, and the world is desperate to experience. She is the Beloved of Christ, his ambassadors of love, beginning within, then outward to the ends of the earth.

1 CORINTHIANS 13:4-8, 13

Love is patient, love is kind. It does not envy, it does not boast, it is not proud. It does not dishonor others, it is not self-seeking, it is not easily angered, it keeps no record of wrongs. Love does not delight in evil but rejoices with the truth. It always protects, always trusts, always hopes, always perseveres. Love never fails.

And now these three remain: faith, hope

*and love. But the greatest of these is
love.*

> *Thank you, Jesus, for showing humanity perfect
> love that casts out all fear. Thank you for giving
> your life and the blood of the new covenant. Your
> life changes everything about my life. I love
> you. AMEN*

I WILL PERFORM IT

> "*Get yourself ready! Stand up and say to them whatever I command you. Do not be terrified by them, or I will terrify you before them. Today I have made you a fortified city, an iron pillar and a bronze wall to stand against the whole land—against the kings of Judah, its officials, its priests and the people of the land. They will fight against you but will not overcome you, for I am with you and will rescue you," declares the Lord.*

JEREMIAH 1:17-19

Don't doubt!

I have spoken over you a powerful word and it is my will and purpose to perform it. Rise up out of fear. Place determination across your chest and wear it as a banner. Fill your heart and mind with the confidence of my commissioning. Lean in and listen as I lead you on this divine pathway.

I will give you the plan, fully, as we walk together. Be attentive to my voice. Turn off the nay-sayers, those voices of doubt. Remain confident in my word, for surely, I WILL PERFORM IT!

AMEN!

 Father, I receive your blessing and will stand for you. It is also my will to perform your purposes in my life. Remind me daily to listen to you and follow hard after you on the divine path. I will not listen to those who speak against the truths of your Word over my life. Thank you, Lord, for your love and affirmation. AMEN

65

DELAY MUST DEPART

> *For the revelation awaits an appointed time; it speaks of the end and will not prove false. Though it linger, wait for it; it will certainly come and will not delay.*

HABAKKUK 2:3

Beloved child, you have tarried in the waiting. Quietly trusting, believing for the promises and answers to your petitions and prayers. When met by delay, you've remained steadfast, never wavering from the truths I have proclaimed.

I've turned my ear toward you when you arrived before the Mercy Seat, beseeching the answers to your longing for understanding of the deferrals. In your pain, as you walked the steady path of obedience without reward, grand preparations were underway, tutoring your soul in groundwork for great treasure. Unbeknownst, you gained profound wisdom of heaven and a deepening knowledge of my presence.

Verily I say unto you, age after age, a number of my children purpose to seek out this rare gift, Wisdom of the Divine. But in their haste, they seek their own ends and thusly have forfeited this Pearl of Great Price. Forerunners surrendered their promises under the daunting pressures of delay, even as answers poised ready, upon the threshold of their heart.

Oh, but alas, my child, you have lingered. Your convictions and faith never wavered. You did not doubt nor relent in your patient petitions. You sought my presence above all else. Learning my language. Pursing my holy fire. Dancing in worship. Singing praise. Surrendering all. Your obedience has unlocked the door. Wisdom and the knowledge of God rushes in.

The long season of delay is closing. The blockage is yours to remove. Ask Wisdom the questions to open the gates, for surely you possess the keys to glory. Invite the knowledge of the Divine to guide your steps.

Speak to delay, "DEPART! The will of My Father is my will."

Now my child, go forth! The season before you will accelerate. Prepare to move quickly. Pray without ceasing. Now behold as the promises come forth, day upon day, freedom upon freedom, healing, health, deliverance, peace, love, joy, and salvations. You are a child of the Divine. Your time in the waiting has granted unto you dominion.

I am in you. You are in me.

Decree this day the delays are broken, engage the angelic. Then stand and behold as the darkness cracks, light breaks upon the horizon. The change you seek will come rushing in as a flood.

Delay is swallowed up in victory and shall be no more. Hallelujah!

Thank you, Father, for your assurances. I will speak to all the delays in my life and I command them to be removed. I have walked with you through the years and I see the faithfulness of your hand upon me. I rejoice that my lingering has prepared me for the season ahead. I declare that I will walk as a child of the Divine and give you the glory as I behold your promises come forth. I speak to the angelic to move now to fulfill all that you have written and prepared for my life. In Jesus' name. AMEN

66

DECISION OF NO RETURN

" *See, I have engraved you on the palms of my hands*

ISAIAH 49:16a

My son, my daughter, the crossroads of no return has presented in front of you. The path diverges and two choices confront your present. A decision of no return, the weightiness of your contemplation bears down. Confusion swirls with threats to overtake your mind in whispers of "what if."

Consequences flash in rapid succession as your thoughts travel every conceivable trail. Fear of the unknown partners with the storm, paralysis is present and prepares to ambush.

BE STILL!

Before me I behold every possibility. I am familiar with your past endeavors, the choices made in boldness and those stepped upon with failing courage. Each setting the direction of your life and choices of great impact and many that were mere blips in a fast-paced lifestyle. I perceive each choice, thought, and prayer spoken. I view each path made possible through your past, present, and future. All in my conscience. Fully aware of your potential and your highest living.

I conceive the chances passed by that offered love and hope and those you seized in the moment which touched your heart and others that brought joy and grace. Each and every choice, every single moment of every day. I AM fully aware of your entire volume of life, in all, the good choices, the failures, the lost potential as well as fullness to the victors gained.

In it all….. I love you.

I love you.

I love you.

You are the choice. I choose you regardless of how far you veer from center, from my presence. I behold your entirety, your entire life. It is love.

I love you with the breadth and depth of eternal understanding. I love you from eternity past and into eternity beyond. I will never leave you nor forsake you. I chose you in love before time began.

Beloved child, choose rightly this path less taken. Walk with me and dream. Ours is an everlasting love that outshines every disappointment, delay, deceit, and distraction.

Believe and trust. I AM love. I AM Abba, your good Father.

I have written your name upon my hand.

 Abba, you choose me, and I choose you. Wrap your love around me in a fresh revelation this hour. Your love is my path and I choose to follow your voice. I know you will direct me on the path, less taken, that I will arrive at the perfect time and the perfect

place. Teach me today how I rest in your love. Reveal to me how to live from peace and rest and to reflect your love to those around me. Thank you, Father. I know you are good and have good for me. AMEN

67

CONTENTMENT

> *But godliness with contentment is great gain. For we brought nothing into the world, and we can take nothing out of it. But if we have food and clothing, we will be content with that. Those who want to get rich fall into temptation and a trap and into many foolish and harmful desires that plunge people into ruin and destruction. For the love of money is a root of all kinds of evil. Some people, eager for money, have wandered from the faith and pierced themselves with many griefs.*

1 TIMOTHY 6:6-10

My child, I perceive your restlessness and your yearning for something different, a changing of a circumstance that appears hopeless or a lost cause. I know that your heart experiences seasons of discontent. But press through these distortions in your faith and prayers. For I am here and your peace is my highest goal for your heart.

Father, I humbly ask for contentment—to be happy, satisfied, and grateful for who I am, where I am, and what I own. Contentment with my accomplishments and peace over my failings, faults, and perceived lack.

I give you, LORD, permission to re-write my thoughts, hopes, and dreams. Write into my life daily awareness of your presence. Moment-by-moment stir my heart to ponder your goodness and perceive the beauty which surrounds me on all sides. Turn my eyes and ears from the lies of the enemy's camp that tell me I am entitled. Free me from the lie that I am missing out, that I am left out, and that God loves others more than me.

In the garden of your presence, I have everything.

My heart is renewed. My soul filled afresh. I'm washed in the blood and cleansed by the water of your Word. You are my contentment, Father. Jesus, You are every perfect relationship. Spirit, you lead me by the still waters and there I will THRIVE. I love you. AMEN

PAST THE VEIL

> *Therefore, brothers and sisters, since we have confidence to enter the Most Holy Place by the blood of Jesus, by a new and living way opened for us through the curtain, that is, his body, and since we have a great priest over the house of God, let us draw near to God with a sincere heart and with the full assurance that faith brings, having our hearts sprinkled to cleanse us from a guilty conscience and having our bodies washed with pure water. Let us hold unswervingly to the hope we profess, for he who promised is faithful.*
>
> *HEBREWS 10:19-23*

Behold! Before me stood an angelic being. Dispatched in response from Abba, Father.

The cry of this season, to the Throne Room of Heaven, "LORD, open my eyes. I want to see past the veil."

Great reverence gripped my soul as this angelic being turned to face me. His power, as a Warrior of antiquity, evident as my hands slightly tremble.

Awe!

His eyes convey the depths of peace of God's realm. Within his gaze, the love of God. The light of the King's dominion.

Instantly his eyes changed. Bloody and wounded with tears of salt and crimson. A fraction of a second, then gone.

Thus, behold the answer to my cry. "God's people cannot see because of the violence, perversion, witchcraft, and debauchery that is allowed into the eye-gate. Seek the balm of healing. Purify your eyes. Bring your vision into the Kingdom and reject what is evil. Restrain the unclean from entering into your heart. Television, movies, music, media. Choose wisely, as the Father has much to reveal in this season of increase. And when you catch a glimpse, you will be swept even higher."

Vanished in a blink. But this message is for God's children.

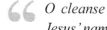 *O cleanse my eyes, Lord. I want to see more. In Jesus' name. AMEN*

THE PERSON JESUS

> *The Word became flesh and made his dwelling among us. We have seen his glory, the glory of the one and only Son, who came from the Father, full of grace and truth.*

JOHN 1:14

Christianity is not a church service. It's not a sermon or a mission trip abroad. It's not a list of wrongs and rights, moral code, and regulations.

Christianity is a person!

A man of flesh and blood who comprehends our struggles. He, who experienced betrayal, condemnation, and persecution, is wildly interested in humanity. He is a person who is concerned about our individual, everyday life, the details, the process, and our purpose.

Christianity is Jesus the Christ. He is alive and with us. He is all around us. He stands and knocks at the door of our hearts, waiting for the smallest opening. And in that singular moment in time when we open that door to this person, he steps in bringing a host of new possibilities. Hope, a fresh perspective, wisdom, discernment. He brings his Father and Holy Spirit.

Jesus is relentless to heal the brokenhearted, our broken mind, failing relationships, and to touch our wounded soul and bodies.

Jesus Christ isn't a myth, just a Bible story, nor a mere religious marquee.

He is a real person who purchased a great number of gifts for all mankind, a life of joy, peace, and goodness. He is a person who loved us before time began and is desperate for us to allow him to love us every minute of every day.

Goodbye religion.

Hello Jesus, the person.

 Jesus, let's spend every minute together today and live life to the fullest. Amen

You are GLORY!

Jesus, when I consider the surrender of your divine nature to come to this lowly planet and live life here as a human, in the flesh, I'm undone. You gave all of you to restore me and my family to life. It's not often that I contemplate the very real struggles you faced in your earthly body. The torture of the cross. Oh, Jesus, let me never forget that you are filled with empathy and compassion as I face difficulties of my flesh. Bless my body today with divine health and keep me from temptation. I choose to live with you today and live to the fullest. AMEN

CHOOSE MEANINGFUL

> *May the God of hope fill you with all joy and peace as you trust in him, so that you may overflow with hope by the power of the Holy Spirit.*

ROMANS 15:13

C hoose meaningful.

Place upon the altar: list, demands, work, dirty floors, and hampers of laundry.

Breathe!

Breathe in the divine gift of pause. Open your soul and perceive my voice breezing through your heart, beckoning; choose the gifts of the ordinary, the mundane.

There are secrets to uncover in the pauses of life. Tiny bits of humor, passels of joy, delight in moments of wonder, beholding your messy-faced baby, murky footprints trailing in search of a jar to lair the ladybug discovered out of doors, and the hopeful eyes of your canine companion awaiting a gesture of devotion, rewarded by an earnest tail wag. Timeless treasures of a lingering kiss—his handsome to your beautiful.

In the simplicity of the ordinary, grasp hope. Slow your striving and be seated on the bench of meaningful. Perceive love. Perceive the whispers of angels as they brush against your ear, disbursing the voices of sorrow, regret, and insecurity.

Choose the meaningful.

Babies, puppies, flowers, bird song, breezes, and the exquisite work of your creative soul.

The meaningful life.

Few catch this abiding gift.

Sit with me and breathe, receive and marvel, then uncover the treasures surrounding you at every turn. My child, you are the meaningful life!

 Lord, my Father in heaven, I choose to stop and focus on you right now. Allow the rush of all the things on my schedule today, fall silent. I'm listening for your voice of love and affirmation. I see you in the everyday beauty of this day. And I choose meaningful. I choose wholehearted living. I choose to honor what truly matters in this life. I choose to love and live in your presence. In Jesus' name. AMEN

71

CAPSIZED TO THE DIVINE

> ❝ *And immediately Jesus stretched forth his hand, and caught him, and said unto him, "O thou of little faith, wherefore didst thou doubt?"*

MATTHEW 14:31 (KJV)

Despondent and exhausted, you give way to the relentless battle and crumple upon the only remaining dry seat in your tiny boat. All strength, abandoned following months of bailing, bucket upon bucket, of the murky darkness pressing into your lifeboat. Now without strength to cope.

Your frantic efforts, heroic. Loud and proud are your accomplishments notwithstanding the numerous challenges to your authority. But today, the words languish distant as the water pools about your ankles.

The unexpectedness of illness, a tiny crack appears, a relentless seepage of doubt in my ability and promise over your life. Followed in succession, financial bludgeons, death, and loss reveal a broken heart and there too, a final gash to the bow, memories of distant trauma bear down, unrelenting.

Beloved, your capsized life is NOT the failure you perceive.

Nay, this IS THE DAY of your rescue. You have reached the end of yourself and the beginning of the Divine. The waters rise, but in the chaos, my armies have arrived. Look up from your remorse and behold the wonder of your Savior.

I've been with you all along. Now look about this sinking facade. BEHOLD my face, my hand, outstretched. Grasp my nail-pierced hand, in this perfection of time. I speak, "Stand and walk with me upon the waters."

Step out of your distortion of control. Behold the rising of the sun and place a steadied foot upon the buffeting waves. At my voice, "Be STILL," the cascades cease their roiling.

The sky breaks with brilliant streaks of light to forge the way. Walk with me and step onto the land of my promise.

You are loved, child of God.

You were never alone.

You will always have a direction forward when you take my hand.

Look about you now, you are standing upon the waters.

Perceive my goodness in the land of the living. Fear not and behold, I am with you always, even to the end of the age.

 Jesus, thank you for your hand. You always arrive right on time. Your miracles surpass my grand expectations. You grasp my hand and lead me out of the torrent of pain and confusion. You are

faithful to set my feet to walk upon the water and triumph over the struggles. I will rest in your faithfulness and give you glory and honor. AMEN

72

THE NESHAMA

> *I in them and you in me—so that they may be brought to complete unity. Then the world will know that you sent me and have loved them even as you have loved me.*
>
> *JOHN 17:23*

Turn your eyes inward and refocus your vision. Look past the smoke, the veneer of hardened masks. Inside of every creature is a part of me. The living breath of God—the Neshama. The spirit of the living God.

I live inside each soul and I am pure, creative light. When you determine your eyes to comprehend me within another, your gaze catches the truest portion of a person. It is their heart. It is their beauty, their hopes, dreams, potential, and joy. Within all humanity and the animal kingdom is an innocence, a portion of undefiled love and truth. It is who I AM. It is the authentic self.

When I look upon my brilliant and creative children, busily going about their day, this is what I perceive, the light that burns within.

My child, each day as you arise, I wait eagerly for your vision to focus. I tarry with you, poised, hopeful that you will engage me and live out of your heart. I watch and stand near with great expectation, urging you to shrug off the lies of fear and doubt. Calling unto you to reach for your destiny with courage. I release blessings of confidence that you would choose to live from your heart and embrace your purposes in creative design, embrace and love your quirkiness, your mess, and your victories.

I stand ready with angelic armies, prepared to assist as you venture into the unknowns of new assignments. And I SHOUT to your enemies—they scatter defeated because today you chose faith over fear. You chose strength in my Son over hopelessness. You chose to love in the face of rejection and abandonment.

This part of me that is you, is your strength, power, authority, and it is your life. My heart is your heart and with my love you are elevated to then perceive the brilliant light within yourself and others. Determine today to move past the smoke screens of those who surround. You will perceive their pain and suffering and also behold the beauty of their divine creativity, hopes, and divine purpose.

When you learn to perceive the light within humanity, the animals, and the natural world, you will catch glimpses of my glory and love. My dear child, love beheld from my vantage point, changes hearts and eternities. Ask me, I'll change your vision and your vantage point will change you. You will engage love. You will experience uncompromised purity and joy which abides in peace.

Oh Father, Christ dwells within me and we are in you. Let me live every day with the understanding that you exist in every heart of humanity. You are the light and goodness within. Father, I invite you to teach me how to perceive your presence in others. Lead me to recognize the light of God that dwells in their hearts. And Father, teach me about how your light reveals the treasures hidden behind human faces. In Jesus' name. AMEN

SPEAK LIFE

> *The tongue has the power of life and death, and those who love it will eat its fruit.*

PROVERBS 18:21

This is the season of Mighty Victory! Breakthrough has been released and my saints are called to speak it forth into the earth. I have prepared the angels for this hour and have expectations for the people of the earth. They will see my majesty, know my love and kindness, and they shall be endued with power from on High to fulfill my will.

Speak life into your circumstances. Stop speaking death. You have the power of life and death in your tongue. Speak life and live!

> *Hallelujah, Father. I speak the words of Jesus. He came to bring life and life abundant. This is my decree this day. Life. Life in my relationships. Life in my finances. Life and healing into my body. Life*

into my home, community, my church, and my future. As a saint, I will carry this banner and release your love and life. AMEN

74

PRAYERS IN THE THRONE ROOM

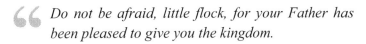

> *Do not be afraid, little flock, for your Father has been pleased to give you the kingdom.*

LUKE 12:32

My beloved child, you were born into a Kingdom. A royal heir with the rights, privileges, and responsibilities fully established before time began. This Kingdom surrounds you and is within. It echoes in your heart and across the ages of eternity with boundless love. My Kingdom is a realm of complete peace, fulfilling joy, and an atmosphere of unconditional acceptance.

My child, perceive this Domain, as it is not far away nor off in the distant future, to one day arrive following a lifetime of faith. Nay, my child, it is present, NOW. Available to my beloved family that you may enter in, behold, and partake.

My enemy, the deceiver of souls, birthed the ultimate deception of distance and separation. He's preached through the lecture halls and the spires of my church a falsehood of ignorance that all which exists is only what is perceived through the five senses of humanity.

My beloved, Nonsense!

Even now the great minds of men and women have discovered and explored other dimensions of the Kingdom of God. There awaits in the halls of science a discerning of more than clouded minds have yet to conceive. Yet, I wait patiently for the findings to unfold. The enemy of humanity's soul is the belief that the earthly plane is all that exists. The frantic pace of life, poverty of soul and pocketbook, employment struggles, conflict, hatred, envy, revenge, bitterness, illness, and fright. These merciless interferences wrench your mind and heart, drawing you into the swamp of a false reality and thus hardens your soul.

BEHOLD! It is within my heart, in this season, this day, this very hour, that my truth shall be revealed. My reality surrounds you at every turn. The heavenly realm is an encompassing, fully alive, glorious possibility to experience in the here and now.

Your prayers of faith are the keys. They are entry into my realm of the "true reality," the Kingdom that was, and is, and is to come. I beseech you—resist the allure to love only upon the earth. It is a conception of trickery. Step this day into my place of rest and peace. My son, Jesus, will lead you and teach you the way. Walk with him. Yoke to him. Behold, you will find me in the Throne Room and discover it is here that your striving ceases, love abounds, redemption of all that is lost is obtained, and the establishing of a life, full of love and adventure, is bequeathed.

Use your keys, beloved, placed within for such a time as this.

 O Lord, I feel the holiness of this moment. With anticipation and fear and trembling, I extend my

hand to receive the key to your glorious Kingdom. Teach me, Lord, how to unlock the gates with this key. It is my purpose to release your Kingdom, to come before your Throne, and to experience the restoration of things lost and stolen. In Jesus' name. AMEN

75

BLESSED TO BE A BLESSING

> *Therefore, as God's chosen people, holy and dearly loved, clothe yourselves with compassion, kindness, humility, gentleness and patience.*

COLOSSIANS 3:12

My child, I bless you to be a blessing. A single moment of kindness bestowed upon a stranger, a friend, your family, is a moment of profound healing and hope. Moments of blessing arrive as you stop, truly lean in, and perceive the people who surround you. Understanding and generosity arise when you choose to look directly into the face of hard living, an outcast tucked away under a sliver of shade behind the convenience store, the forgotten and left behind. The miracle moment converges with grace in a word spoken without judgement to bless with love and provide cold drink, a sandwich, or perhaps a coffee for the commuter behind in the drive-up lane.

One act of kindness purposes to unravel the briars which bind the heart and control the mind. Kindness is a powerful choice, when wisely optioned, wreaks havoc upon offense and hate.

Release kindness and spill out words from a heart of intention—I love you, I'm sorry, I believe you, I stand with you. These are blessings of life and prosperity that liberates a sorrowful soul, revives a marriage, and saves a life.

Bless your home with kind words, bless your children every day, and bless your town or city. Could kindness transform a nation? Dare to believe. This substance of human kindness flows out from the source, pure love from my heart, and it is your secret weapon. I bless you to be a blessing. I am offering you a key to the Kingdom of God. Use it with wisdom and lavish expectation then behold the miraculous that floods your life and love that transforms others.

Father, I receive your blessing to be a blessing. Create in me an awareness when the moment is at hand to bless others with provision, love, hope, and peace. AMEN

76

THE DAWN OF PROMISE

 I saw Satan fall like lightning from heaven.

LUKE 10:18

Behold the dawn of promise. The breaking of the fast releases my hand, afresh.

Your circumstances are reframed in change. Failures of yesterday, cleansed under a crimson deluge, an invigorating hope-spring. Choices of transformation are shaped, prepared. Angelic armies rush in, powerful and readied, awaiting commands of conquer, your voice of missions and rescue.

My child, I AM here, with each morning emergence. I delight that your eyes open, hopeful that you rise in truths and trust, knowing I AM with you and ever before you.

The light of dawn ushers in my voice of redemption of your yesterday, strength for your today, and decrees covering your tomorrow. The morning tide, tranquil, positions the bringing of the hours. Let this moment invite you, serenely, step in. Step out, breathe in the air of nature, beholding the glory of the sky, multifaceted colors, and dimensions. Listen as birds chirp, worship, worship, worship. Holy, holy, holy.

Take heed as Hope whispers gently upon your face. She dances quickly in passing, as a breeze.

My child, your privilege in this brilliant moment, a choice. Lay yesterday at my feet. All your failures, attitudes, sin, fears, and shame. In a single FLASH, crimson, brilliant, light banishes all.

Behold! The Lion of Judah who sits upon his throne! The children of God discover unrealized strength at this dawning. Rise up. Wings of eagles, your birthright. My child, ascend above the storms of chaos, demise, and pain.

Another FLASH! The enemy is decimated, and a download of the Divine is dispatched. Holy strategies for victorious living, dreams restored.

In this dawn's hour, rise, my child, release yesterday.

BELIEVE!

Heighten your today. Meaningful with possibility. Breakthrough at the noonday hour. Overcomer, your destiny. Choose today, my presence, moment-by-moment.

All things are possible for those who believe.

All things are probable.

You are my child, now soar!

 Oh Father, I receive this truth that your promises are new every morning. Great is your faithfulness. I surrender my disappointments and shortcomings of yesterday. Every day is new, and I believe you

have goodness for me all the days of my life. I will live out of this truth as I place my eyes, steadfast upon the Lion of Judah. AMEN

YESHUA, ANOINTED ONE

> *And so it was, that, while they were there, the days were accomplished that she should be delivered. And she brought forth her firstborn son, and wrapped him in swaddling clothes, and laid him in a manger; because there was no room for them in the inn.*
>
> *And there were in the same country shepherds abiding in the field, keeping watch over their flock by night. And, lo, the angel of the Lord came upon them, and the glory of the Lord shone round about them: and they were sore afraid. And the angel said unto them, Fear not: for, behold, I bring you good tidings of great joy, which shall be to all people. For unto you is born this day in the city of David a Saviour, which is Christ the Lord.*
>
> *And this shall be a sign unto you; Ye shall find the babe wrapped in swaddling clothes, lying in a manger.*

And suddenly there was with the angel a multitude of the heavenly host praising God, and saying, glory to God in the highest, and on earth peace, good will toward men.

LUKE 2:6-14 (KJV)

In the quiet before the early light think upon the traditions of Christmas. My child, rise and sit alone with me. Press into my heart and travel with me through the ages, back to a tiny town in the Judean wilderness.

There in the village, Bethlehem, shelters a teenaged, soon-to-be mother, struggling in birth pains throughout the night. Allow your heart to perceive the stalls of bleating sheep. The goats quaking from the cold, huddle nearby. Feel the coarse straw where Mary, the mother of God, rests as she pushes through her labor, hour-upon-hour.

Breathe in the earthiness of the animals, the feed, the dung, and perceive this couple in this humble place as they labor together. The shadows flicker across the roof beams, lit by a single oil lamp.

Finally, the last cry and she pushes forth the child. The King of Kings, the Messiah, arrives into the hands of a young Jewish man, Joseph of Nazareth. He quickly comforts the whimpers of the child, wiping him clean. Resting the child in the trough of animals, he turns to Mary, wipes her face, then settles her with a sip of water. She fades off to sleep.

Wrapped in torn strips from Mary's dress, the child rests. Joseph ponders the destiny of this tiny baby within his hands. He prays. He offers thanks to the heavenly Father as he gazes into the perfect face of a babe that is the Chosen One, The Christ, who has come for all people.

All of heaven responds in a culmination of majestic worship and praise echoing throughout the centuries. The angle chorus, hallelujah! The heavens rejoice. Time splits in two. Hope returns. Joy and freedom are proclaimed over the people. Devils flee.

The love of God is alive upon the earth.

Immanuel—God with us!

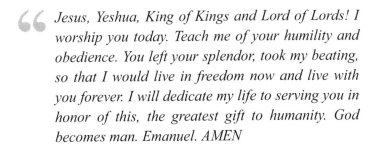 *Jesus, Yeshua, King of Kings and Lord of Lords! I worship you today. Teach me of your humility and obedience. You left your splendor, took my beating, so that I would live in freedom now and live with you forever. I will dedicate my life to serving you in honor of this, the greatest gift to humanity. God becomes man. Emanuel. AMEN*

78

BEAUTY OVERCOMES BRUTAL

 Do not be overcome by evil, but overcome evil with good.

ROMANS 12:21

L ife rushes and pushes and there are days when living feels beyond difficult, nearly impossible.

Trauma overwhelms and there is little room in our society for one to be weak, unable to cope.

The wickedness of men results in a brutal world—where children cry alone at night. Mamas fear, dads retreat. Sleeplessness becomes the soul's companion.

Yet, a mystifying reality exists in tandem.

Beauty.

Beauty is sheltered within a kind word received in perfected time.

Beauty is recognized in the wrinkled and worn face of an old woman who prays endearingly for her grandbabies.

We behold beauty when a young man gazes across a room to catch a glimpse of his beloved returning his smile in an intimate understanding of familiar.

Beauty in the words: I forgive you.

Beauty in the brilliant facets of grace.

Beauty in a million lights tossed across the expanse of a cloudless night sky and a melodious song of a dove through the morning mist.

Breathtaking as the spray falls gently on a child's upturned face from the ocean waves. Beauty in a thousand sunsets and an oversized, harvest moon.

Love of a mother.

Kindness of a stranger.

First sip of coffee on a chilly autumn morning.

Playtime with daddy.

Beauty surrounds on all sides yet endlessly competes against the relentlessness of the brutal.

Hope versus hopelessness.

Healing versus pain.

Good versus evil.

God versus all else.

Every part of our soul longs for, is fighting for, the beautiful. And it *is* ours to behold and to live within.

It's a choice, every day, in everything.

It's our Redeemer, the giver of life, love, and the creator of beauty—Jesus.

You decide which to live within. Choose the beautiful and pray for the brutal. Choose wisely, my child.

 I choose beauty, Father. I choose Jesus. I choose to see the unending beautiful moments you create. I will look to the good and reject the evil. I will pray beauty forth over my home and family. I will stand upon faith and never cease to put brutality into the grave. Thank you, Lord, for beauty. I choose to see you in beauty and my heart rejoices! AMEN

79

PONDERING FAITH

66 *Since what may be known about God is plain to*
them, because God has made it plain to them. For
since the creation of the world God's invisible
qualities—his eternal power and divine nature—
have been clearly seen, being understood from
what has been made, so that people are without
excuse.

ROMANS 1:19-20

An atheist dreamt he died and found himself before God as it was his appointed time to give an account of his life.

A nod from the King and the man began: I lived a life as a good man. I never killed anyone. I obeyed the laws. I supported causes of the people. I studied at the university and then taught science to the betterment of thousands of souls on earth.

I looked for you, God, to reveal yourself at times in my life. I did wonder if you might exist. After my wife left me, I considered going to church, but I never made it.

I studied and read many books that assured me you were a myth, a creation of society that needed a deity to cling to. But alas, no, I never read the Bible. It was said that it was an old book and flawed work that I was made to feel embarrassed to consider relevant. And now I know it was true.

God nodded.

But God, I lived my entire life, 80 years. Why in all that time didn't you reveal yourself to me?

God replied: Bring to your remembrance each morning when you walked out your front door on your way to work and you gazed up into the sky to consider the weather. It was then you looked upon my brilliance. Within the bluest sky you beheld my presence. When you patted your dog's head and chuckled at the enthusiastic tail wagging, when you shuffled in at night, when you filled your lungs with the fragrance of fresh rain upon your city, my love was in it. When you beheld the majesty of the mountain peaks of snow, the grandeur and power of a mighty waterfall, the breadth of the ocean, intricacies of the human body and the precision of the science you taught each day to your students, I was in it. You saw my face every day.

I was around you everywhere.

Then the man spoke: But God, what about the ugly, the brutal, the utter evil that I witnessed?

The Father: Yes, my enemy works to ensnare, deceive, harm, and kill. But you had a choice to make each day.

Choose Me. Choose hope.

Choose the lies and one day die in them.

Then the man woke.

What this day shall you choose?

Look for the living God. He is all around you.

Smile, because he cares for you.

 Father, this is indeed a conversation that brings into sharp focus the daily choices that come before me. I choose you. I choose to focus on the living God and bring your truth and reality into this world. I pray for every unsaved person within my sphere of influence. Lord, please allow me the opportunity to represent you well that they will find salvation in your son, Jesus. AMEN

DEFEAT DELAY

> *Declaring the end from the beginning, and from ancient times the things that are not yet done, saying, "My counsel shall stand, and I will do all my pleasure."*
>
> *ISAIAH 46:10 (KJV)*

The spirit of delay has settled over many of my children. The dreams and realities, released in the last season appear lost, unattainable. This sly demonic effort slipped into the minds of my children in a momentary fight with fear and doubt.

But BEHOLD! I vanquish the devices of this devil and demand his surrender. This year is the release of the Acts 2 Church. I have determined my people WILL bear witness to the display of my power and purpose. No longer will delay destroy the dreams I have set into the minds and hearts of My Church.

My child, resist!

The surrender of this dream is not your destiny. Declare today your faith and trust in me with all thine heart; and lean not unto thine own understanding. In all thy ways acknowledge me and I shall direct thy paths (Proverbs 3:5-6).

Speak out your prayers of supplication, repentance, and worship. Continue on in bold faith. The season of trial by delay will prove the powerful positioning of my purpose. In what appears as delay is truly the defeat of a muted enemy. I AM your good Father. I AM smiling upon your heart of intentions for my Kingdom. The swells of prayers from the secret place arise in contrails into the heavens. All of Glory hears your faith. Your petitions and praise rise in offerings. Jesus, placed as a sacrifice of love, tipped the Scales of Justice.

Blessings pour forth, angelic support—fulfillment of my Word and promises now burst upon you. Believe and receive for I WILL accomplish everything that I please!

SO BE IT!

 In the name of Jesus, my Savior, I receive this powerful word. "So be it" is also my cry. What you have determined will come to pass in my life. I shout to the devils of delay, BE GONE! It is my inheritance to receive your blessings. I honor you, Father and I believe. I will watch as you fulfill your faithful word in my vision. AMEN and Hallelujah!

81

THE COURT OF THE JUST

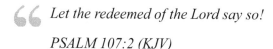 *Let the redeemed of the Lord say so!*

PSALM 107:2 (KJV)

A great turning is approaching. My sons and daughters, have tarried in willful intercession, seeking an audience in the Court of the Just! The pleading of the Saints arises hour-by-hour, coalescing upon the Scales of Justice. Prayer-upon-prayer, ascending; directing purpose, calling the prodigals home. Speaking to the wayward spouse and the many who remain lost in the confusion of addiction and fear.

The demands of the warriors of prayer upon my hand of love and holiness compel my heart toward the nations. The iniquity of the unrighteous draws upon it, the light of revelation. Exposure of the malice once concealed in throes of dark incantations, debauchery, and broken souls.

Ah, my children.

I feel the brokenness and I receive your yearning prayers for the rescue of hearts who are bound in irons, labels, deception, witchery, confusion, rebellion.

Alas, my faithful intercessors, the glorified prince!

The King! Mighty Prince, Jesus, adorned in battle armor, fire blazing across the skies from his countenance. His mount, brilliant steed of white and might, readied.

A shout, "Let the redeemed of the Lord say so!"

Saints of old, antiquities past, join the many living and readied upon the earth. The time— imminent. Let the advancement of the Armies of The Living God commence.

Lives restored. Identities rescued. Children returned whole. Families healed. Pain abolished!

Let the redeemed of the Lord say so!

All are welcomed. All are loved. All are safe. All are my children.

It is time!

All hail King Jesus!

 I speak these words in unison with the angels, "Let the redeemed of the Lord say so!" Father, thank you for the redemption of my life. For my rescue from shame, pain, and insignificance. Lord, I will shout of what you have done for me. I will speak of you and your goodness to those around me. I will shout of your love and grace. I love you, Father. AMEN

82

SONS OF COURAGE

> The thief comes only to steal and kill and destroy. I came that they may have life and have it abundantly.

JOHN 10:10 (ESV)

I sense a profound stirring in the atmosphere—angels whisper in expectation, preparation. The compelling knowing of God is turning the page in this moment of history. His voice, deep with pride and powerful determination:

It is time for the men to arise!

My sons of my Kingdom, your destiny awaits. I will delay no longer, that which I now establish and return to you, your honor. I will recognize your wisdom, quiet strength, integrity, and righteousness.

Far too long, the men of earth have been assaulted, stifled with heavy burdens. They carry tremendous responsibility as they shoulder profound obligation—family, workplace demands, the fulfillment of their commitments, small and large. My sons face shaming in the public square and are minimized by the voice of wickedness. They pray in the midnight hour; a solemn tear trails their face. They beseech and bring me their worries, placed before the Mercy Seat; their marriage, their beloved children, and pleading for wisdom and relief from the debts and financial perils that threaten.

Silently and yet with stubborn constitution, my sons determine themselves to stand up straight and carry the lives of those they love upon their chest, within hearts.

To my sons, I behold your fortitude, your courage. The battle deepens with greater intensity, and the provocative surrounding is palpable. But I AM moving, and I AM on the move. I AM restoring eroded positions and long-forgotten destines. I AM returning the stolen peace to your heart and supplying warriors from the heavens to shore up your finances, strengthen your marriage, and fortify your homeland.

Determination is my scepter. It is raised to extinguish the word curses spinning across the airwaves that have shackled my sons in anxiety and inaction. Today I release this great company of the masculine to dream again. I bestow their freedom to laugh with delight, play in enthusiasm, love with passion, and reflect my glory.

Arise Kingdom sons! The time grows short. Gather the families, walk in my truths. Bring in the lost and forsaken. Forgive freely and love with all your might.

Great is your assignment.

GREAT is your reward in this hour.

I bless you, my sons. Well done. Well done!

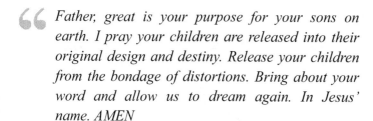

Father, great is your purpose for your sons on earth. I pray your children are released into their original design and destiny. Release your children from the bondage of distortions. Bring about your word and allow us to dream again. In Jesus' name. AMEN

ALIGN MY DESIRES

> *And be not conformed to this world: but be ye transformed by the renewing of your mind, that ye may prove what is that good, and acceptable, and perfect, will of God.*
>
> *ROMANS 12:2 (KJV)*

Lord, align my desires with yours.

Today, align my thoughts with yours. Align my work to yours. Align my heart to your heart. Seal my life to be wholly dependent upon your life.

Align my energies and efforts to what you are doing on this earth in this season. Align the love in my soul to your love. Align my heart to love others.

Align my eyes to see what you see, to perceive as you perceive. Align my dreams to be birthed from your dreams about me and for me.

Align my wisdom to the wisdom of heaven and to reject the voice of worldly enticements. Align my pursuit of you to be holiness, kindness, compassion, truth, and righteousness.

Align myself to be a leader to others and that I would lead in humility and love. That others would then align their love to your presence.

Align my worship to your heart, to bring you honor and glory. Align my words to be words that become a well-spring of hope to myself and others.

Align my mind to your mind that I think only what you think about me.

Align my every minute of every day to offer you thanksgiving for the richest blessings of provision, protection, and grace.

In Jesus' name. AMEN

84

ARMIES OF THE LIVING GOD

" *Then I looked and heard the voice of many angels, numbering thousands upon thousands, and ten thousand times ten thousand. They encircled the throne and the living creatures and the elders. In a loud voice they were saying:*

"Worthy is the Lamb, who was slain, to receive power and wealth and wisdom and strength and honor and glory and praise!"

Then I heard every creature in heaven and on earth and under the earth and on the sea, and all that is in them, saying:

"To him who sits on the throne and to the Lamb be praise and honor and glory and power, for ever and ever!"

REVELATION 5:11-13

There is a rumbling in the distance. Behold! The Armies of the Living God!

The Cavalry of Heaven prepared for this hour. Millions upon millions surging forward. Bound to earth in power and holy assignment. The Sabers of Faith are prepared, blades refined through flames of fierce fire. Placed within the hands of my people.

Satan's hordes shriek. Decimation is eminent. The strike of the blade shreds Deception's restraints and shackles of fear. The sludge of black exploitation and filth melts, as of wax, back into the bowels of the earth as the Sword of Truth slashes hatred, lies of false identities.

Ancestral sin and curses are crushed in an instant. Punishing addictions are thrown down, back into the pit forever. AMEN! Witchcraft falls to the ground, powerless, as the people are released from hypertension, arthritis, endocrine system interruption, and disease of all manner. Evil and illness are severed from the human body, mind, spirit, will, and emotions with one powerful blow of the Sword of Life, wielded by the hand of the Lamb of God.

In this hour, mandates and positions are reestablished! Destinies are reshaped. Honor and dignity restored. Pain is thrashed to the ground and FREEDOM SHOUTS! GLORY!

THE KING IS HERE!

He is riding in leading the Armies of the Living God. Listen intently, you will perceive his approach. Wait expectantly and believe! Then become part of the legions, step into the Kingdom mission, set the captives free and begin with me! Hallelujah! AMEN!

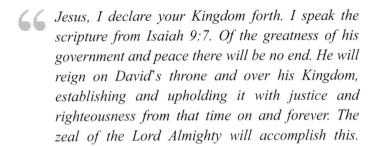

Jesus, I declare your Kingdom forth. I speak the scripture from Isaiah 9:7. Of the greatness of his government and peace there will be no end. He will reign on David's throne and over his Kingdom, establishing and upholding it with justice and righteousness from that time on and forever. The zeal of the Lord Almighty will accomplish this. Amen and AMEN.

85

A MERE WHISPER AND FORGIVENESS ARRIVES

> *But he said to me, "My grace is sufficient for you, for my power is made perfect in weakness." Therefore I will boast all the more gladly about my weaknesses, so that Christ's power may rest on me.*

2 CORINTHIANS 12:9

My child, in a brave step of possibility, you raised your head above the dark waters of shame and regret. I perceived the shallow, barely audible gasp when you whispered, "God, help me." Deep within your fearful and broken heart, the desperate words quickened unto my hearing.

I distinguish the battles waged against the beasts of addictions, fears, failures, shame, and inadequacy. Your pleadings for rescue, a taste of freedom, only to relapse in the abyss of a punishing taskmaster of uncontrollable cravings, carnal, seductive—illicit.

Your voice above the dark waters, distant and fading, pleading for hope to fully rescue with permanent fire and redemption. Do not fear to seek my forgiveness over and over for I understand the depth of your troubles and the evil that tempts. You fear that you surrendered once again and this time the boundary crossed as though forever.

Never!

My character is forgiveness. My name is Redemption.

Cry out to me again.

Ask. Forgive me, Father. Save me, Father. Heal me forever, Father.

My grace is sufficient for you (2 Corinthians 12:9). My words are healing. My love is freedom. My heart receives you over and again. Approach with boldness, my Throne of Grace and receive mercy and grace in your hour of need (Hebrews 4:16). Confess the grievances of your addiction, attraction, lost identity, your shame, and failures. Assign them over to me to heal, transform, and legislate your Kingdom freedom.

The blood of my Son, Christ Jesus, speaks a better word... (Hebrews 12:24) ... Redemption, fullness, joy, healing, salvation, forgiveness, eternity, and wholeness.

My hand is outstretched—grasp and draw near. Woman, where are your accusers? I do not condemn you (John 8:10).

 Father, thank you for revealing the depths of your unending grace. I receive the forgiveness and the assurances you will enable me to rise above my weakness. I know your strength shines upon my humble surrender. I surrender all, Lord. Have thine own way. In Jesus' name. AMEN

86

A BREAKTHROUGH OF FAITH

> *Surely goodness and mercy shall follow me all the days of my life: and I will dwell in the house of the Lord forever.*

PSALM 23:6 (KJV)

Something is about to break. A paradigm, a transition—change. Looming, thick awareness.

The pressure is building, seismic. The tension is tangible.

This awareness of impending change leading to contention within isn't born of disaster. You are recognizing the birth pangs of reformation, intrinsic of heaven. A change, a repositioning of significance.

Breathe through the transition.

Fix your gaze wholly on me. In the pain and confusion that swirls about you, let my years of faithfulness be your strength and truth.

The moment of revelation draws nigh. And your laboring in prayer hastens the end. You are in the midst of transition and the struggle is great. Your efforts intensify, anxiety is prone.

Grip my hand as you push forward. FEAR NOT! For great is your reward.

You will see the goodness of the Lord in this new season. Well done, good and faithful servant; you were faithful over a few things, I will make you ruler over many things. Enter into the joy of your Lord!

 Father, I surrender my fear concerning changes that will arrive in my life. I step into faith and belief that you are my good Father and have prepared a year, overflowing with breakthroughs in my faith life, my family, and every challenge placed before me. I will prayerfully look to you to guide me with your wisdom through the months ahead. And I thank you for your faithfulness, love, provision, and grace that have followed me all the days of my life. In Jesus' name. AMEN

87

THE OFFERING OF FIRST FRUIT

   Honor the Lord from your wealth

   And from the first of all your produce.

   PROVERBS 3:9

I AM your future.

Offer me your first fruits each morning. Prayer and intimacy before your phone, before all distractions. The sacrifice of your first in your day moves my hand within your struggles. Arise and join me in my chamber of meeting. Let us sit together and become one with one another.

This is the seat of rest. From this position, the greatest counsel and wisdom flows. This seat is where I AM. From the seat of perfect rest, your heart will settle, your striving cease, and your concerns fade away.

The Spirit of Wisdom arrives with books, scrolls, and blueprints readied for your purpose. The foe is defeated and defied from this place and position. Weapons of chaos and fear are washed away by the Living Water as peace flows gently from my hand upon your mind.

I offer you this unusual and rare gift. Enter the chamber of the Most High and experience Shalom. I will teach you to rule and reign from the seat of rest and the armies of hell will not defeat you.

Your desire and hunger for more of me has opened up the gate to the chamber of the Most High and from this seat of rest you are revered among the angelic. Honored child, you are offered a seat at the table of the divine council.

Well done, my child, well done.

 Father, thank you that you have opened the way into the chamber of your presence. You have offered me a rare and special honor to be seated in rest and to rule from the council of heaven. I am ready to leave the earthly striving behind and sit in perfect rest. I will speak peace and your purposes into my life today and know that I am living from rest and peace. Thank you, Lord. AMEN

88

DANCE ACROSS THE YEARS

>> *You turned my wailing into dancing; you removed my sackcloth and clothed me with joy, that my heart may sing your praises and not be silent. Lord my God, I will praise you forever.*

PSALM 30:11-12

Welcome to the greatest adventure.

This promise is given, you will never be left wanting, bored, or disappointed within our tandem dance across this life. I've prepared each step, each day, as a unique gift for your heart and healing unto your soul.

Pursue the day always attentive to my voice. Listen for the clues to search out the treasures I've placed into your day for your delight. They are hidden joys in the smile of a stranger. You will experience happiness and wonder though a random book, a scripture verse, or in the beauty of a single snowflake or the swirling of an evening breeze.

Allow me to be your delight and adventure, your purpose and plans. I will not disappoint nor leave you wanting. Surrender is the key to the greatest adventures. Offer me your all, then watch as everything changes and gates of the impossible open unto you.

This dance, my beloved child, was conceived before time began. It's my great pleasure to watch you twirl across the years with grace and love as you fulfill your callings and purposes.

 Lord, allow me to take in the reality of this tandem dance. You haven't placed me on earth to dance alone but have held my arms as you lead into greater understanding and powerful living. This dance is my grand adventure and I look forward to each day as you lead me into new places and experiences. I treasure the truth that your desire is to gently lead me into my purpose and callings. This stirs my heart with love and excitement for tomorrow. Thank you, Father. AMEN

89

WHERE LOVE ABIDES

> *Trust in the Lord with all your heart and lean not on your own understanding; in all your ways submit to him, and he will make your paths straight. Do not be wise in your own eyes; fear the Lord and shun evil. This will bring health to your body and nourishment to your bones.*

PROVERBS 3:5-8

Why have you contended alone? You have yet to conceive that I carry concern and emotion over all aspects of your life. Every day of your years are numbered with details and seemingly small choices. Insignificant moments that appear as non-thoughts as you live upon this earth.

These small meaningless choices, however, accumulate into larger impactful decisions. These decisions over time, often take on their own strength and lead to a path of regret, and at the extreme, destruction. Begin with me in the small things. Even the littlest of moments and choices of your conscious thought. These are the mustard seeds of faith.

Retrain your thoughts to include me. I will reshape the small decisions so that they become great opportunities in the place of frustration or disaster. Speak to me throughout the day. Join me to seek my voice, my perspective.

It's in the small that the great is birthed. It's the tiniest of life that becomes a legacy. Try me in this and behold the truth. When I become your all-in-all, you have stepped over into the mustard seed faith, the realms of all things possible. This is where I dwell. You are welcomed into this realm of the eternal where blessings flow and love abides.

> *Oh Lord, my Father, I want this intimacy. Teach me to surrender beginning in the small, the mustard seed choices of faith. I know this is true that the small choices, when well guided, will blossom into bold opportunities, provision, and joy with laughter. Train my mind to ask you, Father, about choices and to learn to follow your prompting when you answer. My obedience opens the miraculous. Your voice is all I desire, Lord. Your voice is all I need to live in triumph, joy, and peace. In Jesus' name. AMEN*

90

WELL DONE, CHILD

Listen, I tell you a mystery: We will not all sleep, but we will all be changed— in a flash, in the twinkling of an eye, at the last trumpet. For the trumpet will sound, the dead will be raised imperishable, and we will be changed. For the perishable must clothe itself with the imperishable, and the mortal with immortality. When the perishable has been clothed with the imperishable, and the mortal with immortality, then the saying that is written will come true: "Death has been swallowed up in victory."

"Where, O death, is your victory?

Where, O death, is your sting?"

The sting of death is sin, and the power of sin is the law. But thanks be to God! He gives us the victory through our Lord Jesus Christ.

Therefore, my dear brothers and sisters, stand firm. Let nothing move you. Always give yourselves fully

> *to the work of the Lord, because you know that*
> *your labor in the Lord is not in vain.*

1 CORINTHIANS 15:51-58

Child of my heart, you have waged the war. Crossing the great gulfs and territories of opposition, equipped only with your sword and armor, your angels, and my presence. You stood in the fire as a barrier against the giants that once overran your land. You battled for your family with passion and you swung the sword of the Lord for strangers along the way.

You stood up, faced squarely, your own demons and gained victory. Then you learned to share your victory over darkness freeing others from the chains of oppression.

You have stepped into maturity as a beloved son or daughter of God. You stand now in a season of victory over the world's lies and temptations. You have gained the crowns of life; the Overcomer crowns now rests upon your brow.

Today, you hold the Key of David, the gate is open, and you are summoned and welcomed into the Father's council. Your faith in the Messiah, Yeshua, my son, is reflected in your life and words. Your prayers move the mountains before you as you step into greater conquests to redeem the promised land for others and set the captives free in the name of Jesus.

You shine as bright as the noonday sun and all of heaven rises with honor when I speak your name. Child of the Most High God, enter your rest. You are worthy. You are adored, loved, and a gift to my heart.

You carry great sway with the King. Welcome to my table and to life of the Divine. Well done, child, well done.

Oh Father, I gratefully and thankfully throw this crown to your feet and worship you. Your goodness and love have changed me into a new person in Christ. I will spend all of my life sharing your heart with this world and all of eternity in thanksgiving and worship.

You are great and greatly to be praised. I love you, Father. AMEN

MINISTRIES OF LYNN DONOVAN

Lynn Donovan
THRIVE in Faith

LynnDonovan.com

———

SpirituallyUnequalMarriage.com

READ LYNN'S OTHER BOOKS

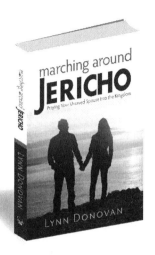

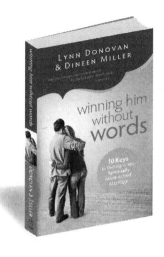

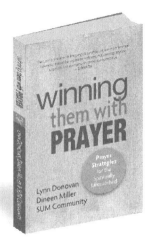

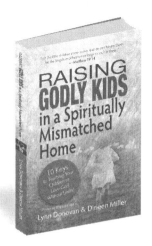

Made in the USA
Columbia, SC
31 May 2021

38566679R00140